World
NEW ORLEANS

Pableaux Johnson
with
Charmaine O'Brien

WORLD FOOD New Orleans
1st edition

Published by
Lonely Planet Publications Pty Ltd ABN 36 005 607 983
90 Maribyrnong St, Footscray, Victoria 3011, Australia

Lonely Planet Offices
Australia Locked Bag 1, Footscray, Victoria 3011
USA 150 Linden Street, Oakland CA 94607
UK 10a Spring Place, London NW5 3BH
France 1 rue du Dahomey, 75011 Paris

Photography
All of the images in this guide are available
for licensing from Lonely Planet Images.
email: lpi@lonelyplanet.com.au

Front cover: *Chef preparing meals at Nola Restaurant on St Louis Street,
French Quarter, New Orleans*
Back cover: *A long cool Pimm's Cup, Napoleon House, New Orleans*

Published
November 2000

Although the author and publisher have tried to make the information as accurate as possible, they accept no responsibility for any loss, injury or inconvenience sustained by any person using this book

ISBN 1 86450 110 3

Printed by
The Bookmaker International Ltd.
Printed in China.

About the Authors

Pableaux Johnson is a food and travel writer who splits his time between the oyster bars of Southern Louisiana and the barbecue joints of Austin, Texas. Following a largely misspent youth in New Iberia, Louisiana and countless culinary migrations, he recently returned to Acadiana and resides in a renovated church in nearby St Martinville. Pableuax is a regular contributor to the *Austin Chronicle*, *Texas Monthly* magazine and the CitySearch online network. In what passes for free time, he eats his way through the world's great food cultures and maintains the travel food website, 'www.bayoudog.com'.

Charmaine O'Brien completed a hotel management degree, then decided that becoming a good cook was her next aim. The usual apprentice route didn't appeal so she learned the ropes by holding a never-ending dinner party. A couple of years of relentless entertaining later, she launched a successful catering and food consultancy business. The discovery of Reay Tannahill's *Food in History* led to a passionate interest in food history. She has terminal wanderlust and her exploration of the world's regional foods has taken her to the dinner tables of every continent.

About the Photographer

Jerry Alexander provided most of the photographs in this book, with other Lonely Planet photographers providing the balance. The photography credits are on page 280. Jerry is a highly credited food & travel photographer with extensive experience working in South-East Asia, particularly Thailand. When he's not travelling around the world – leaving behind a trail of crumbs from eating his props – Jerry lives in California and tends to his vineyard in the Napa Valley.

Acknowledgements

From Pableaux: collective thanks to my many eating buddies, traveling companions and partners in crime. Special thanks go to Georgia Flynn and Chris Poche for the constant hospitality and underground tips (did I mention the Sazeracs?); Ruthie and George Bilbe for acting as reliable sources; Carla and Joe Mouton for the cross-generational fact-check; Kevin Rioux for the coffee and cake. Sisters Charlotte Paulsen and Elaine Johnson worked the phones and Annie, Will and Molly Bates giggled when necessary. Kate Lowrey helped with a Northern perspective, and Stu Wade kept the asylum on speed-dial. Robb Walsh dispensed valuable unsolicited advice and Steve Este valiantly bartended on command. Mary Minor Hebert gave the first push. Ariana French gave much-appreciated love and support and rolled her eyes at the appropriate times. Most of all, this book is dedicated to the memory of my mother Carmelite Hebert Blanco and her late parents – Lorelle Seal Hebert and A. Leon Hebert – who taught me the value of eating, storytelling and laughing around the family table.

From Jerry: A photographer is keenly aware that good images are seldom made alone. The hospitality of New Orleans and Louisiana is on the very short list of great places on this planet. I fell in love with it all! Some particular thanks to my wife, Loma, who made it work, Jason Giles, Bruce Margan and Bonnie Warren for opening doors, Rob & Kevin (B&W Courtyards B&B), Allen & Marine (Mandevilla B&B), Coerte & Marjorie (Bois des Chenes Inn), Guy & L.J. (Jefferson House

B&B), Gary (Seale's B&B). Many thanks also to Paul Prudhomme, Roy Lyons, Anne Kearney, Joann Clevenger, Antony Uglesich, Ann Christian, Andrew Jaeger, Acme Oyster House, Greg Sonnier, Commander's Palace, Mathilda, Prejean's, Rocky & Karen, Dave McIhnny, the folks at Melrose, Celeste, Wallace Johnson & family. And to those I've left out please know I'm forever grateful and hold your part of the world in a new light!!!

From the Publisher

This first edition of *World Food New Orleans* was edited by Patrick Witton and Lyndal Hall, and designed by Brendan Dempsey of Lonely Planet's Melbourne office. Natasha Velleley mapped and Lara Morcombe proofed and indexed. Matthew Anning edited the dictionary. Peter D'Onghia oversaw the book's production. Valerie Tellini of Lonely Planet Images coordinated the supply of photographs and Brett Pascoe managed the pre-press work on the images. Andrew Tudor provided technical assistance.

Sally Steward, publisher, developed the series and Martin Hughes, series editor, nurtured each book from the seeds of ideas through to fruition, with inimitable flair.

Warning & Request

Things change; markets give way to supermarkets, prices go up, good places go bad and not much stays the same. Please tell us if you've discovered changes and help make the next edition even more useful. We value all your feedback, and strive to improve our books accordingly. We have a well-travelled, well-fed team that reads and acknowledges every letter, postcard and email and ensures that every morsel of information finds its way to the appropriate people.

Each correspondent will receive the latest issue of Planet Talk, our quarterly printed newsletter, or Comet, our monthly email newsletter. Subscriptions to both are free. The newsletters might even feature your letter so let us know if you don't want it published.

If you have an interesting anecdote or story to do with your culinary travels, we'd love to hear it. If we publish it in the next edition, we'll send you a free Lonely Planet book of your choice.

Send your correspondence to the nearest Lonely Planet office:

Australia Locked Bag 1, Footscray, Victoria 3011
UK 10a Spring Place, London NW5 3BH
USA 150 Linden St, Oakland CA 94607
France 1 rue du Dahomey, Paris 75011
Or email us at: talk2us@lonelyplanet.com

contents

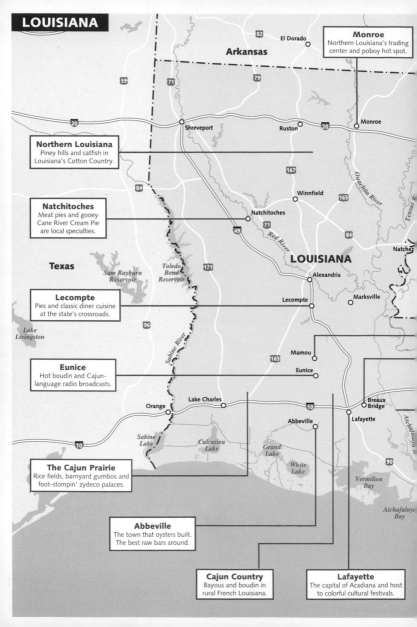

LOUISIANA

Arkansas

El Dorado

Monroe
Northern Louisiana's trading center and poboy hot spot.

Monroe

Shreveport

Ruston

Northern Louisiana
Piney hills and catfish in Louisiana's Cotton Country.

Winnfield

Natchitoches
Meat pies and gooey Cane River Cream Pie are local specialties.

Natchitoches

Texas

Sam Rayburn Reservoir

Toledo Bend Reservoir

LOUISIANA

Alexandria

Marksville

Lecompte
Pies and classic diner cuisine at the state's crossroads.

Lecompte

Lake Livingston

Mamou

Eunice
Hot boudin and Cajun-language radio broadcasts.

Eunice

Lake Charles

Breaux Bridge

Orange

Abbeville

Lafayette

Sabine Lake

Calcasieu Lake

Grand Lake

White Lake

Vermilion Bay

The Cajun Prairie
Rice fields, barnyard gumbos and foot-stompin' zydeco palaces.

Atchafalaya Bay

Abbeville
The town that oysters built. The best raw bars around.

Cajun Country
Bayous and boudin in rural French Louisiana.

Lafayette
The capital of Acadiana and host to colorful cultural festivals.

Ouachita River

Red River

Sabine River

Tensas

Natchez

Atchafalaya R.

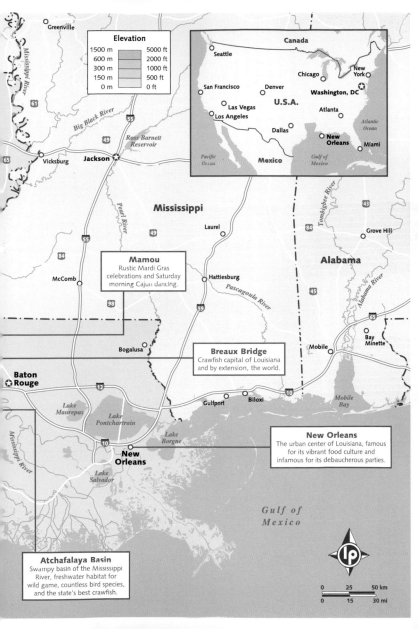

Elevation

1500 m	5000 ft
600 m	2000 ft
300 m	1000 ft
150 m	500 ft
0 m	0 ft

Greenville

Mississippi River

Big Black River

Ross Barnett Reservoir

Vicksburg

Jackson

Pearl River

Mississippi

Laurel

Mamou
Rustic Mardi Gras celebrations and Saturday morning Cajun dancing.

McComb

Hattiesburg

Pascagoula River

Tombigbee River

Alabama

Grove Hill

Bogalusa

Breaux Bridge
Crawfish capital of Louisiana and by extension, the world.

Mobile

Bay Minette

Baton Rouge

Lake Maurepas

Lake Pontchartrain

Gulfport

Biloxi

Mobile Bay

Lake Borgne

New Orleans
The urban center of Louisiana, famous for its vibrant food culture and infamous for its debaucherous parties.

Mississippi River

New Orleans

Lake Salvador

Alabama River

Atchafalaya Basin
Swampy basin of the Mississippi River, freshwater habitat for wild game, countless bird species, and the state's best crawfish.

Gulf of Mexico

(Inset map)

Canada

Seattle

Chicago

New York

San Francisco

Denver

U.S.A.

Washington, DC

Las Vegas

Los Angeles

Atlanta

Atlantic Ocean

Dallas

New Orleans

Miami

Pacific Ocean

Mexico

Gulf of Mexico

0	25	50 km
0	15	30 mi

Among cities of the United States, New Orleans is an historical enigma, a cultural anomaly, and a non-stop culinary celebration. Founded by the French, governed by the Spanish, and eventually absorbed by the United States, the city has a many-layered history and pleasantly schizophrenic personality. Musically, it's the birthplace of jazz, a stronghold of blues, and a place where energetic brass bands roam the streets. The city is also host to the country's most famous (and infamous) carnival, Mardi Gras. But what really fuels this city is its vibrant food and drink culture. Freshly caught redfish swim in butter sauces derived from the French tradition. Dark and flavorful Creole **gumbos** feature wild duck and winter oysters. Even workaday dishes like **red beans and rice** reveal something of the city's evolving culinary history.

In fact, it's been said that any stay in New Orleans is best measured in meals instead of days. You can start any morning with sugary **beignets** (deep-fried pastries) and steaming cups of **café au lait** (coffee with milk) at a local cafe, or indulge with high-dollar brunch at one of the French Quarter's old-line Creole restaurants. Lunch can find you munching your way through a gargantuan **poboy** (French-bread sandwich) or savoring a bowl of sherry-spiked **turtle soup**. Afternoon hunger pangs may lead you to one of the city's oyster bars for a dozen raw mollusks washed down with frosty beer. By the time dinner rolls around, you'll be wondering how the locals survive the city's manifold temptations.

But the local culinary experience doesn't stop at the city limits, as there are rich and wide-ranging foodways both within and beyond the Crescent City. New Orleans' indigenous Creole cuisine is a New World take on classical French traditions, mixed with the varied influences passing through the mighty Mississippi's southernmost port city. Cajun food, the trademark cuisine of the 'frontier-French' Acadian population has also added to the mix, but its heart lies in Southern Louisiana's Cajun Country. And dishes from the American Southern country-style and Soul Food traditions have made their way downriver from Northern Louisiana's cotton country.

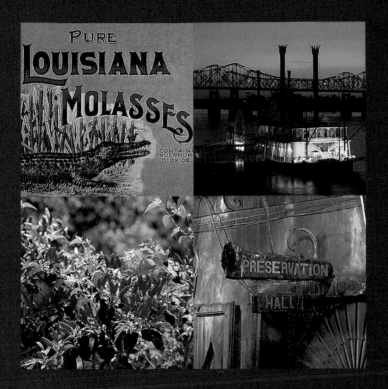

the culture of louisiana cuisine

As it was, is, and ever shall be – New Orleans' food is varied, rich, and exciting. With its historically crucial river and as a thriving maritime port, New Orleans has always been an important gathering point for culture and cuisine. Just as the essence of Gallic culture is found on the dinner plate, so it is in the Crescent City, the largest French cultural outpost in the Americas.

Creole, Cajun & Soul

When we speak of modern-day New Orleans food, we're actually speaking of the unique mixing of three dominant cooking styles – Creole, Cajun, and Soul Food – commonly associated with both the city and the state of Louisiana. The first two are native to predominantly French Southern Louisiana while both Southern Country-style and Soul Food (generally referred to as Soul Food), is an import of sorts – a combination of adapted British cuisine and African influences that dominates most other states in the American South.

Buttery-rich, refined and sophisticated, **Creole cuisine** is the food of the city and the delicious legacy of the city's French heritage. Dishes including the delicate **poisson en papillote** (fish cooked in parchment paper) and **shrimp remoulade** are prime examples of this Continental-turned-native cuisine – local ingredients interpreted in a style that reflects French roots while incorporating contributions of the other cultures that passed through the port city. On the whole, Creole cuisine is smooth and rich, with a tip of the hat to the sauces and formal presentations of the French motherland.

THE BUTTER THE BETTER

The rich cuisine of New Orleans is undeniably and unapologetically butter based. Nearly every Creole dish – from appetizer-portioned crab claws to decadent bourbon-sauced bread pudding – is surrounded by a glorious pool of melted butter. If you see the word 'sauteed' on a menu or in a Louisiana recipe, the words 'in butter' can't be far behind. Baskets of hot, crunchy French bread are served with pats of the smooth, sweet spread. Substituting margarine would be considered borderline criminal.

In these increasingly fat-phobic times, it's the buttery richness of the dishes that make palates rejoice and waistlines expand for travelers and locals alike.

Rustic, flavorful, and bold, **Cajun food** is the food of the country – in this case, the Southern Louisiana marshes, bayous (tributaries) and prairies west of New Orleans proper. Often mistakenly attributed to New Orleans, Cajun food has its physical and cultural roots with the rural settlers from maritime Canada rather than Parisian aristocrats. Eighteenth-century refugees from the French Canadian province of Acadie (now known by its British name, Nova Scotia) brought their unique frontier cuisine and adapted it to the remote areas of what is now alternately called Acadiana,

The Chart House, the French Quarter, New Orleans

Staff at the Praline Connection serving fried chicken, peas & cornbread

Acadian Louisiana or Cajun Country. (With time, the name 'Acadians' was shortened to 'Cadien' and then Anglicized to the modern term 'Cajun'.) The long-simmering single pot dishes (such as crawfish étouffée, shrimp jamba-laya, roux-based gumbo) reflected the survival-oriented frontier traditions of the Acadians – simple foods based on the varied bounty of the land – and were different from the refined foods common to New Orleans' established French Creole population (see the Regional Variations chapter).

Soul Food – as well as its closely related cousin, **Southern country-style food** – is a variation of the English cuisine indigenous to the Anglo-American Deep South, a region that ironically lies directly *north* of largely coastal French Louisiana (see the boxed text French Louisiana vs the Deep South later in this chapter). Broadly speaking, both schools of cooking are derived from British cuisine adapted to indigenous ingredients and the cooking techniques of African slaves and African American hired cooks. The often-blurred distinction between the two schools is the quality of the raw ingredients. As a general rule, Southern country-style cooking starts with the pick of the crop or carcass, and Soul Food stews up the rest.

Both of these styles reflect the edible legacy of the Deep South's planta-tions and subsistence farms along with the often complex racial and ethnic history of the Deep South. Common examples of these styles include crispy fried chicken, okra smothered with tomatoes, collard greens cooked with salt pork, hearty yellow cornbread and fluffy raised biscuits. The common configuration for a typical Southern country-style or Soul Food meal is the 'meat and three', a single serving of meat accompanied by three different vegetables. Most common in the rural towns and agricultural centers of Northern Louisiana, these styles floated downriver and left a delicious mark on New Orleans as well.

In New Orleans, these three major cuisines mingled with countless other cuisines and international influences, making it one of the most vibrant food cultures in the United States.

Biscuits in a cast-iron skillet

SOUL FOOD

In early days, African slaves may have been preparing meals for wealthy white families but they certainly weren't eating the same food. The white families ate the hams of the pig and the slaves made do with the ribs, offal, feet and skin. The white folks ate vegetables such as turnips and the slaves got the green tops. They were given molasses (used as a flavoring) cornmeal and whatever else was leftover or considered second rate.

Slaves were usually permitted to keep their own small patch of herbs and vegetables as well as a few chickens, and out of this they created their own family meals. Food was often deep-fried in pig fat, which was readily available. They stewed poor-quality meat for hours to tenderize it and develop its flavor. While the slaves had little choice in the foods they ate, they came to develop a rich, hearty, delicious cuisine – including greens, chitterlings, cornbread and ham hocks – we now know as Soul Food.

Soul Food is very popular in the American South, and you will find it in city and country restaurants. It is not indigenous to the region like Creole and Cajun food, and while you will find Soul Food all over the southern US, the version you eat in Louisiana will have more pepper, spice and garlic.

Charmaine O'Brien

History

Any quick reading of New Orleans history shows that this city's heritage is both varied and multilayered. New Orleans was colonized in the 18th century by the French on a site originally settled by Native Americans and briefly governed by the Spanish. The thriving port played host to countless ethnic groups from Europe, the Americas, slave territories of Africa, Caribbean ports, and Asian fishing grounds. Refugees from British Maritime Canada, post-revolution Haiti, and post-war Vietnam all found homes in this laid-back but traditionally cosmopolitan city.

In the early 1700s, French settlers and traders founded the post of Nouvelle Orleans (now Anglicized to New Orleans) near the mouth of the Mississippi, North America's largest river. Within a short time, the newly formed city became a major center of the New World's river and ocean trade and an important conduit for French culture in the Americas.

When the French arrived, they found Native American peoples – such as the Attakapas, Chitamacha, and Houma nations – successfully living off the land. Mother Nature had supplied the Native Americans with an abundant pantry, and they introduced the Europeans to salt and freshwater creatures such as oysters, crawfish, crabs, shrimp, turtle, speckled trout, and catfish; wild game such as pigeon, rabbit, dove, squirrel, duck and deer; and plantlife such as wild greens, onions, berries, beans, pumpkins, squash, watermelon, peaches and corn (maize). The French learned how to pound leaves from the sassafras tree into a flavorful powder which they called **filé** (see Sassafras & Filé in the Staples & Specialties chapter).

The infusion of new ingredients into the settler's French cuisine gave birth to the Creole food associated with the city. The rich sauces and pureed soups common to the homeland were adapted to the fresh ingredients of the New World.

Creole cuisine was also affected by other strong cultural influences; often home-cooks were not French, but African. As affluent descendants of European French settlers, colonial Creole families in New Orleans often kept slaves and it was African women (and *their* descendants) who did the cooking. While fine Creole ladies were not taught to cook, it was their duty to ensure that meals were on the table. A Creole wife might equip her African cook with a menu of the finest classical French dishes, but it was up to the cook to interpret those dishes or add her own touches. Eventually families became accustomed to this African-influenced cooking and a new cuisine evolved (see the boxed text Bowl Full of History later in this chapter.)

New Orleans' native cuisine grew more distinctive as the city and its trade connections grew. Ships arrived from French colonies in the West Indies and barges floated in from cotton plantations in the Mississippi's fertile river delta. Under the political control of France, New Orleans

Close up view of a paddle steamer, New Orleans

CULTURE

became an active shipping center, but in the 1760s New Orleans played host to a second ruling power of significant cultural influence, the Spanish. During their 30 years of control, the Spanish vastly improved the city, establishing a centralized marketplace (the current-day French Market) and offered rural land grants to the wandering Acadians establishing a proto-Cajun homeland and making the now-famous cuisine possible. In the aftermath of the French Revolution, a wave of former nobles also took refuge in New Orleans.

The early 19th century saw the French regain temporary control of Louisiana, Napoleon's quick sale of the Mississippi River basin to the fledgling United States, and official US statehood in 1812. These rapid-fire developments brought Anglo-American settlers (and their trademark foods) into Northern Louisiana. Other groups flocked to New Orleans, which was by then a crucial river port and point of entry into the US. Free black settlers from Afro-Caribbean Haiti and Santo Domingo came to the city, as did slaves from Senegambian West Africa. Italians (mostly from Sicily) settled here in record numbers, bringing their distinctive dishes and adding **red gravy** (spiced tomato sauce) to the developing Creole culinary style. Freed slaves from other American states made their way here following the

Striking colors of the French Quarter, New Orleans

CULTURAL REGIONS

Arkanas

Shreveport

Mississippi River

Texas

Alexandria

Mississippi

Alabama

LOUISIANA

Lafayette

BATON ROUGE

New Orleans

Gulf of Mexico

- Northern Louisiana (The Deep South)
- Acadiana (Cajun Country)
- New Orleans

American Civil War. Germans arrived and set up wheat farms outside the city. Irish fleeing the Great Potato Famine populated the neighborhoods near the French Quarter and contributed to the city's distinctive 'Yat' accent (which is very similar to New York City's native dialect of 'Brooklynese').

Intervening years saw New Orleans and its cuisine develop into their distinctive modern-day manifestations. The Crescent City is now an active modernized river port in a traditionally poor section of the United States. During the 20th century, improved railroad lines and the discovery of oil helped develop the economy of Southern Louisiana and connect the culturally secluded Acadians (now called Cajuns) with New Orleans and 'the American world'. New ethnic groups – including a late-century wave of Vietnamese immigrants – came to the city and made their contribution to the city's diverse living cuisine.

In the past 20 years, New Orleans' food scene has also been affected by a group of very influential non-residents – the travelers and tourists that pump millions of dollars into the economies of New Orleans and the rest of Louisiana. New Orleans draws travelers from around the world to its many historical attractions, seductively decadent celebrations and renowned restaurants. As a result, the city has become a hotbed of traditional

CREOLE IN CONTEXT

Whether you are talking about New Orleans' urban cuisine, historical ethnic groups, living cultures, or tangy blood-red tomatoes, the word Creole will probably come into play. Derived from the Spanish word *criollo* (meaning 'native to a locality'), Creole can take on many different meanings depending on its context. Here are a few:

• The native food of New Orleans, Creole cuisine is a unique form of French cooking developed with New World ingredients and foreign influences specific to the Louisiana port city.

• Historically, the term was used to delineate a particular lineage in colonial New Orleans – the direct descendants of the French and Spanish settlers of the region.

• Creole also describes the French-speaking descendants of Afro-Caribbean free people of color (*gens de couleur libres*) who fled the West Indies and settled in New Orleans and rural Southern Louisiana.

• Linguists use the term to describe languages where a mixed-language dialect is used as a group's primary tongue, as is the case in some rural communities where a patois of English and French is spoken.

• A modifier used to describe certain Louisiana foods, as in juicy Creole tomatoes and coarse-grained Creole mustard.

and contemporary cuisine. The Cajun Hot movement of the 1980s triggered an urban boom in all foods Cajun (and the mistaken association of New Orleans with Southern Louisiana's rural Acadian culture). Neon-lit chain restaurants and low-quality eateries now cater to the tourist trade and sport tacky souvenir t-shirts and overpriced servings of faux Cajun jambalaya. The same is true in the rural reaches of Acadiana, where gaudy tourist spots and matching billboards have sprung up along major highways. However, the tourist spots haven't replaced the 'real deal' – both the city and countryside have plenty of authentic establishments that do justice to Louisiana's living food traditions.

The important thing is that you jump mouth-first into the vibrant cuisines of New Orleans and the other parts of Louisiana that feed the city both literally and metaphorically. Your personal exploration of Louisiana's living food cultures will shape and be shaped by your own tastes, experiences, and love of the region. After all, there's no single way to experience the city, the swamp, or the countryside – if we're lucky, we can eat our own personal path through the land.

How New Orleanians Eat

For the average resident of New Orleans, food is much more than simple sustenance – it's a hobby, a constant topic of conversation, and a borderline obsession. As in other sections of Louisiana, food (with its corollary activities of procuring, cooking, and eating) is the collective passion at the core of New Orleans' distinctive local culture.

As a rule, the people of New Orleans eat big, often and with a sensual enthusiasm that borders on the sexual. Discussions about transcendent foodstuffs – from a homemade **sauce piquante** to flaky pastries from a local bakery – can trigger moans of ecstasy and howls of delight, even from sedate, well-mannered matrons. Average portions for any meal varies from large to gargantuan, which accounts for the enhanced girth of many locals. Travelers have commented that in New Orleans, there's really no such thing as a light meal.

FRENCH LOUISIANA vs THE DEEP SOUTH

The problem with cultural boundaries is that they don't often show up on gas station roadmaps. If it were common practice to show these often-crucial lines instead of the more convenient political frontiers, Louisiana would look very different indeed.

In cultural terms, Louisiana is divided into three distinct cultural zones: New Orleans, the biggest port and independent city state; the Cajun region of Acadiana; and Northern Louisiana, the only section that can be accurately called 'The Deep South'.

Geographically, of course, Louisiana *is* part of the Deep South – a term often applied to the group of states from coastal South Carolina to the eastern border of Texas. Culturally, though, Louisiana differs significantly from the other states in the region (Alabama, Georgia, Mississippi and South Carolina), which all share a host of common cultural features. States of the Deep South were settled by English immigrants, Scotch-Irish settlers, and slaves brought over from the coasts of West Africa. They have been historically rural, agricultural and often poverty-stricken. And in terms of religion, they are dominated by conservative strains of evangelical Protestantism.

All these characteristics are found in Northern Louisiana, but they don't reflect the Franco-Catholic cultures of New Orleans and Cajun Country. French Louisiana's colonial experience separates it from the Anglo-American 'Bible Belt' both in terms of history, culture and demographics. And it's the separation that gives French Louisiana its unique cultural flavors (see the Cultural Regions map earlier in this chapter).

CULTURE

Locals taking time out in a cafe, Lecompte

In the city, restaurant culture reigns supreme, mostly because there are so many outstanding restaurants in which to indulge. Unlike other American cities, where the exceptional restaurants occupy the upper end of the cost spectrum, New Orleans has a well developed mid-priced and even low-end restaurant scene, which is accessible to people from all walks of life. Many of the city's trademark dishes – overstuffed seafood poboys and garlicky muffulettas – were invented and popularized by the poorer segments of the city's population (see Poboys and Muffulettas in the Staples & Specialties chapter). Industrial workers and wealthy businessmen alike know their way around New Orleans' menus. Because much of the city is employed by the tourist service industry, the populous keeps abreast of restaurant news and the comings and goings of prominent chefs and respected cooks.

New Orleans adheres to the standard American pattern of 'three meals a day' in practice, if not in spirit. The classic morning meal of fried **beignets** (warm, sugar-dusted French doughnuts) and **café au lait** (coffee with milk) is a leisurely indulgence, but gallons of hot coffee are more the norm. Whether it's a full eggs-and-bacon diner meal or a quick bowl of cereal, breakfast is a relatively small deal compared to the midday meal – called 'lunch' in the city and 'dinner' in the rural reaches of Northern Louisiana. The traditional break in the workday is a time for social gatherings and business dealings, and a chance to sample the city's restaurant fare at cut-rate prices. Friends meet regularly to try out new contemporary Creole joints downtown. Rumors among office mates of 'the best oyster and artichoke soup' can inspire a field trip for sampling and arguing purposes. The city's economic and social strata mingle at lunch counters and tiny diners across

Jazz brunch at the Court of Two Sisters, New Orleans

town, comparing notes on the day's special – a rich bowl of crawfish bisque or a roast beef poboy dripping with rich brown gravy. Taking the evening meal (referred to as either dinner or supper) at a restaurant is generally reserved for special occasions, even if it's to commemorate the fact that it's Wednesday night.

Many family traditions are observed with large meals in the home, preferably with a multi-generational group in attendance. Often there are special dishes prepared for family gatherings such as baked ham for Sunday dinner, jambalaya for a sister's birthday, or duck and sausage gumbo to celebrate a successful hunting trip (see Celebrating with Food and the Home Cooking & Traditions chapters). These gatherings are also the hallmark of home cooking in Cajun Country and Northern Louisiana (see Cajun Country and Northern Louisiana the Regional Variations chapter).

Impulsive between-meal snacks are relatively common, since you have to have *something* to go along with your morning coffee. And your afternoon coffee. And all the cups of coffee in between. Tourists in New Orleans often have to find time *not* to eat, since the temptation to sample local specialties is ever present. In Cajun Country, cracklins (deep fried pork skins) and links of boudin (pork and rice sausage) are always popular savory snacks. The afternoon pause for 'pie and coffee' is popular in small town diners across the state.

NEW ORLEANS BRUNCH

If you live in New Orleans, Sunday brunch can be an important family tradition. The historic concept of brunch was shaped by the demands of the Catholic Church that required the faithful to fast from midnight Saturday until after mass on Sunday.

By the time you left the church not only had you been spiritually refreshed, but you were also mighty peckish. But it was too late for breakfast and too early for lunch, so brunch was devised as an in-between sort of meal and popularized by such old line Creole restaurants as Brennan's and Commander's Palace. Grillades and grits (grilled beef or veal slices braised in tomato sauce and served with cooked mush of coarse-grained hominy) is a classic New Orleans brunch dish. Jazz bands were added to the mix, and the tradition of the 'Jazz Brunch' is now a common Sunday morning tourist draw. New Orleans may not be the devout Catholic city it once was, but brunch remains a very popular meal among tourists who can afford the pricey egg dishes and morning cocktails referred to as 'eye openers' (see Eye Openers in the Drinks chapter).

CULTURE

A BOWL FULL OF HISTORY

Pull up a chair. Have a bowl of gumbo. Me, I make my roux as dark as Mississippi mud. I like wild duck, andouille sausage and okra in my gumbo. I serve it steaming hot over rice with a bottle of Louisiana pepper sauce and a baby food jar full of homemade **filé** (crushed sassafras leaves) on the side so you can sprinkle. Sprinkling gives you something to do while the soup is cooling. Another thing you can do while you're waiting for your gumbo to cool is to look deep into the bowl for a minute and consider the strange history of this dish.

Gumbo existed long before the French 'discovered' the Mississippi. When the Europeans and their African slaves first arrived, the natives served them a catch-all stew thickened with powdered sassafras, also known as filé powder. Powdered sassafras has a slimy consistency when it is mixed with liquids, and it reminded the West African slaves of a stewed okra dish from back home. The word 'gumbo' comes from the Umbundu (West African) word for okra, *ngombo.*

This connection between *ngombo* and the Louisiana stew called gumbo has caused all sorts of arguments. Some food writers speculate that gumbo without okra isn't really gumbo. Others argue that there are many authentic gumbo recipes that don't include okra. And all of this silly recipe chatter misses the far more important point. The Africans were interested in the slimy native American dish because it resembled a ceremonial dish of their West African religion. Whether it contains okra or not, the dish we now call gumbo was probably invented as a Voodoo sacrament.

How the okra actually got to the Deep South is also something of a mystery. According to food authority Waverly Root and the authors of most cookbooks, okra was brought to the Americas by African slaves. The captive Africans secreted okra seeds in their hair or inside their ears during the long journey to America, we are told.

As I strolled barefoot through the okra patch in my garden one sticky morning a couple of summers ago, I started wondering about these accounts of okra's arrival in the New World. I split an okra pod open with my thumbnail and squirted a few round seeds into my palm. The okra seeds were about 2mm in diameter and the idea of having a few rattling around in my ear made me wince. As I walked back to the kitchen with my okra pods, I tried to imagine myself a captive West African being lead away in irons by white men with whips and guns. How would I react? Seething with anger, weeping with sorrow and screaming in rebellion all came to mind. Sticking some okra seeds in my ear did not.

"I've never met a scholar who believed that the slaves really brought seeds with them to the New World. The notoriously brutal conditions imposed during capture, transportation and sale must largely rule this

out," Dr Robert Voeks, Associate Professor of Geography at California State University at Fullerton, told me on the phone. These legends about slaves bringing okra seeds and other plants to the New World come from Candomblé, Santeria and Voodoo folklore, Voeks told me.

Candomblé, Santeria and Voodoo are New World religions derived largely from Yoruba traditions that originated in what are now the West African nations of Nigeria, Gambia and Benin. In its various guises, the West African religions have remained nearly intact on this side of the Atlantic. For several centuries, they have coexisted with Catholicism in a complex system in which African deities and spirits are syncretized with Catholic saints.

During his field work in the Bahia region, Dr Voeks was initiated into a terreiro, or holy house, of Candomblé in order to learn more about the religion's fascinating ethnobotany. In his book, *Sacred Leaves of the Candomblé* (University of Texas Press) Voeks describes the practices of Candomblé herbalists, priests and priestesses, who employ some 500 different kinds of plants in their rituals, celebrations and healing ceremonies. Foods like okra, black-eyed peas and yams are among the plants that have religious significance.

The deities of the Condomblé religion are called Orishas and each has a unique personality and favorite food. Shango, the Orisha of thunder, is a womanizer and predictably enough, he is fond of goat. Yansan, the wind spirit, likes the black-eyed pea fritters called *acarajè*. On the feast day of each Orisha, worshippers prepare the spirit's favorite food.

Carur, or okra stew, is the food of the Ibeji, the twin gods of procreation and reproduction. The festival of the twin deities is also called *Carur,* and on this event the consecrated okra dish must be prepared. But there are other times when an Orisha's dish must be prepared, such as when someone falls ill or needs assistance. In such times an Orisha can be summoned by placing its favorite food on the supplicant's head. In the American Deep South, okra or gumbo, probably took the place of the sacramental food eaten at the time of the Ibeji festivals and used in fertility ceremonies.

As for the legend of the okra seeds in the ears, Dr Voeks has done a lot of detective work on the mystery of how West African medicinal herbs and native plants came to be transplanted to the New World. He has shown that in some cases, freed slaves actually returned to Africa and shipped the missing magical ingredients of their religions back to their friends and families. But in the case of okra, yams and black-eyed peas, there is a much simpler explanation. The slave traders brought them over, Voeks says.

The African slaves were supplied garden plots and expected to grow their own food on the cotton plantations. Bringing over the plants that the slaves already knew how to grow was simply the most expedient

The grave of Voodoo Queen Marie Laveaux, New Orleans

way to keep them fed. And it made good business sense to keep the slaves healthy. A West African staple, okra is a fair to good source of calcium, potassium, vitamin A, and vitamin C. It also supplies about seven grams of protein per 100 calories. It is high in fiber, very filling and prolific in the tropics where it thrives during the heat of the summer when other green vegetables wither.

Like many religious myths, the Voodoo legends of slaves bringing okra seeds to the New World in their ears caught on because they express a larger truth. Okra was a sacred food for the Yoruba people of tropical West Africa, and thanks to Yoruba slaves and their descendants, okra became an important part of African-American cuisine.

The African slaves of the Deep South were accomplished practitioners of two distinctly different cooking styles. In their own homes, they cooked approximations of traditional West African dishes based on yams, rice, spinach, black-eyed peas, okra and the offal and meat scraps they were given by slave owners. But while working in the kitchens of the plantation houses, they learned a completely different style of cooking.

As citizens of a French colony, the early plantation owners of Louisiana decorated their elaborate manor houses with French fabrics and furnishings and outfitted their kitchens with French cooking equipment. The kitchens were generally small sheds built at some distance behind the plantation houses to reduce the danger of fire and to cut down on the heat in the house.

In French cooking, the most common thickener for soups and sauces is the flour and butter mixture called roux. It can be lightly cooked for a white sauce or bechamel, or cooked longer for a darker brown sauce. In French Louisiana, wheat flour was a luxury that had to be imported from Europe. The African slaves mastered the French style of cooking and in the process created many of the elegant stuffed and breaded fish, fowl and meat dishes of the Creole tradition.

As time went by, the French-trained African-American cooks began to invent new combinations. Eventually dark roux found its way into the gumbo pot and the Creole version of gumbo appeared. Using a variety of fish and shellfish along with tomatoes, a rich gumbo was created that was reminiscent of the French dish, bouillabaisse, and sufficiently elegant for the plantation houses and New Orleans mansions.

But the evolution of gumbo wasn't really complete until the Cajuns arrived. The Acadian diaspora began in 1755, when the English pushed French settlers off the Canadian island of Acadia and renamed it Nova Scotia. Acadians emigrated to French colonies all over the world, and a great number of them ended up in Louisiana. They inhabited the frontier country surrounding the Atchafalaya swamplands, well beyond the French civilization of New Orleans.

Okra and peppers

The Cajuns were a littoral people, used to a lifestyle of subsistence fishing and hunting. They were joined in the swamplands of Louisiana by native Americans, adventurers and frontiersmen from the United States and Creoles, or French-speaking Africans. By combining their rough-and-ready French Acadian wilderness cooking with the African-influenced Creole style, the Cajuns created yet another folk cuisine and yet another approach to gumbo. And it is this Cajun gumbo that is the one we know best.

With their love of wild game and spices, the gumbo that the Cajuns created was entirely different from the African okra stew or the Creole seafood soup. It might contain fish, fowl or sausage or all of the above. It could be argued that what the Cajuns did was to bring gumbo full circle, back to its native American roots as a highly-spiced, catch-all stew.

Thickened with roux, studded with okra and topped with a slick of filé powder, the bowl of gumbo on the table in front of you is an ancient native American dish named after an African vegetable. It is a Voodoo sacrament, a traditional French stew and a wild French-Canadian amalgamation, all at the same time.

Have a bite. It's spicy, eh? Now when you hear people say the culture of Louisiana and the Deep South is a gumbo, you will know what they're talking about.

Robb Walsh
Robb Walsh writes about food for the *Houston Press* and is a commentator for National Public Radio. His column A Matter of Taste' appears in *Natural History* magazine.

Etiquette

There are no real surprises with etiquette, as eating here is generally a relaxed affair. If you know how to eat politely in a restaurant or at home with your in-laws, you'll be fine. If you are eating at someone's home a small gift and words of praise for the meal will see you invited back.

You are unlikely to encounter any unusual eating utensils. Knife, fork and spoon are the standard table setting, with special utensils added for fish, soups and salad courses in restaurant settings. But eating here is a robust activity and in informal situations, nobody shies away from getting down and dirty with their food. For example, it's impossible to eat an overstuffed poboy without wrestling the huge sandwich into submission – a very difficult task for dainty eaters. Likewise, if you are eating boiled seafood, dive in hands-first and watch your companions for the correct behaviors.

Fresh French bread, delicately wrapped in white cloth, accompanies many restaurant meals, and standard local procedure is to break it with your hands, even in the swankiest establishments. Don't worry about the crumbs – the locals certainly don't.

'NO SMOKE' SIGNAL

Traditionally, New Orleans hasn't been particularly rigid in its attitude toward smoking, considering it an expected after-dinner pastime. But in keeping with recent US trends, many places in New Orleans are now enforcing strict indoor no-smoking policies designed to eliminate carcinogenic 'second hand' tobacco smoke. Some of the older restaurants will maintain a separate smoking section where diners can light up after their meal. If you happen to dine in a smoke-free environment, but do want to smoke, just make a beeline for a nearby barroom, where clouds of blue tobacco smoke are always in style.

In home situations, serving food from a communal dish (also called serving 'family style') is common. The food will be placed in the middle of the table for you to help yourself. Make sure you use serving utensils and not your personal cutlery to take food from a communal dish. If you are adding sauce to your meal when serving family style, wait until you get your portion on the plate before you add the sauce. If you are dining with a family, they may say grace before the meal. If this is unfamiliar to you, just bow your head and follow the family's lead.

staples
& specialties

In terms of ingredients and culinary creations, Louisiana and its culinary capital of New Orleans are unrivaled lands of plenty. Fertile soil and wetlands provide an abundance for the pantry. Cooks here have used native and imported ingredients to create specialties that are found throughout Louisiana and reach their peak in the Crescent City. And there's no better way to learn about this region's food than a course of study led by the senses and stomach. So dig in.

CAJUN COMES TO THE CITY

In the early 1980s Louisiana chef and Opelousas native Paul Prudhomme introduced Cajun cooking to the wider world with **blackened redfish** – his not-so-traditional signature dish. Dipped in cayenne-heavy spice mixture and quickly seared in a cast-iron skillet, this dramatic preparation attracted the attention of chefs and the media alike. The problem was, it had no real precedent in traditional Cajun cookery. Cajun grandmothers scoffed openly at "that man serving burned fish to those poor people who don't know better."

Then the inventive executive chef at Commander's Palace (one of New Orleans' flagship Creole restaurants), Prudhomme devised the flash-searing technique and single-handedly bridged the gap between Louisiana's city and country cuisines. The 'Cajun Hot' movement of the 1980s followed and passed into American food history, but blackening still survives as the most visible vestige of the national trend.

Seafood

As the port capital of a coastal state, New Orleans has an amazingly rich seafood tradition. Many of the staple dishes of Louisiana cuisine use creatures yanked from the state's intricate wetlands – saltwater, freshwater and brackish marshes – and most of these end up in the kitchens and restaurants of the Crescent City. Direct intervention from the Catholic Church, in the form of the fish-on-Fridays tradition, has also contributed to Louisiana's healthy seafood industry.

Fish

Many of the classics of New Orleans Creole cuisine are straightforward preparations of local fish such as snapper, speckled trout, pompano and flounder. (Straightforward, meaning with the addition of copious amounts of butter.) **Trout meuniere** features delicate fillets of the Gulf fish lightly dusted in flour, pan fried in butter and topped with lemon butter sauce. A simple grilled pompano is transformed into **pompano Ponchartrain** with the topping of sauteed lump crabmeat (see Crabs later in this chapter). Other schools of Louisiana cooking use the local finfish as the cornerstone of their respective repertoires. Cajun cooks turn redfish or snapper into flavorful dishes like **courtboullion** (a robust, spicy tomato-based dish rich with peppers and spices). Dredged in cornmeal and deep fried, the catfish becomes a stalwart of the Soul Food pantheon. Wherever a fisherman has a good day on the boat or at the fishing hole, deep-fried fish show up at the table.

STAPLES

CATFISH – FROM TRASHFISH TO TREASURE

Ugly bottom-feeders. Mud-filled trash fish. Until recent years, the catfish – the de facto trademark fish of the American South – had a bit of an image problem.

With its natural freshwater habitat in muddy rivers and ponds, the omnipresent catfish (*Ictalurus furcatus*) vacuums the watery floors for tasty morsels and in the process also ingests a fair amount of sludge, pesticides, and post-industrial goop. Traditionally, the catfish has been the food for the poorer people. But thanks to modern farming techniques (aquaculture) the whiskered wonder is back in relative fashion. The taste of the fish was transformed when they were farmed in ponds and fed compressed grain pellets. For a new breed of water farmer, catfish are an attractive economic proposition since they are easy to breed and grow quickly. The catfish is now akin to an aquatic chicken; it's widely available, cheap, easy to cook and has a fairly neutral flavor.

Crabs

Any crab eaten in New Orleans is likely to be the indigenous blue crab, a tasty crustacean prized by Native Americans and settling Europeans alike. During peak crab season (April to October) these tasty shellfish are available fresh-boiled at informal restaurants and boiling points across the state (see Boiling Points in the Where to Eat & Drink chapter). The rest of the year, sweet chunks of peeled meat (usually described as 'lump' crabmeat) make their way into everything from starter salads to gooey, doubly rich **crab au gratin**, bubbling with cheese and breadcrumbs.

Crabmeat in its various forms (flawless lump and slightly less desirable claw meat) also forms flavorful fillings for stuffed eggplant and deep-fried **stuffed crabs** (where stuffing is eaten in a hard, pre-scooped crabshell). Creamy dips, crunchy **crab cakes** (fried patties of crab, breadcrumbs, and seasonings) and seafood **gumbos** (see Gumbo later in this chapter) also benefit from the crab's decadent flavor and texture.

At summertime crab boils, piles of the fresh-cooked animals present a challenge for the novice peeler (see Boiling Points in the Where to Eat & Drink chapter). In its purist form, boiled crab is *anything* but an impulse food. The gloriously messy 'peel and eat' process requires a quick lesson in crustacean physiology and considerable patience, even for experienced eaters. But don't be deterred by the prospect of pointed claws, shrapnel-like shards of shell and 'lung removal' – once you learn your way around the crab's meat-filled nooks and crannies, you'll be hooked. If you're not used to eating crab and would like to avoid the possibility of spiking yourself and missing all the best bits of meat, ask for a crab-shelling demonstration from your host or fishmonger.

Travelers fortunate enough to visit during the earlier part of crab season can indulge in the classic spring-summer seafood specialty – soft-shelled crab. As part of its molting process, the blue crab sheds its shell three or four times a year for the first few years of its life. If caught more or less in its birthday suit, the crabs can be eaten whole, shell and all (see the boxed text opposite). Soft-shelled crabs are usually pan-fried with a browned butter sauce or stuffed with various seafood mixtures.

Patrons of the New Orleans Jazz and Heritage Festival can enjoy the soft-shelled crab in its popular **poboy** incarnation (see The Poboy section later in this chapter and the boxed text Sultry & Sugar-dusted, Welcome to JazzFest in the Celebrating with Food chapter). Once fried, these crabs are cut in half and inserted into a crusty sandwich roll in the legs-up position for easy snacking on the crispy appendages. Jokingly referred to as the **bug poboy** or **spider sandwich**, it's a great way to taste the season's best in between stages.

LIVE NUDE CRABS – THE SOFT SHELL PROCESS

As part of its life-cycle, the blue crab molts its shell several times a year. To do this, the crab gorges itself, takes in a lot of water and its existing shell bursts. While the crab goes on its instinctive eating binge, it draws calcium out of its hard shell and stores it to assist in growing another.

When crabs are in this critical between-shells stage, farmers remove them from the open waters and place them in special underwater holding pens. Crabs are cannibals and when one molts and is at its most vulnerable, others will eat it, given the chance.

Then comes the labor-intensive watch-and-wait process. A white line on the last segment of the hind paddle means that the crab is two weeks from molting. These crabs are placed in a pen and checked weekly. When the white line has changed to pink the crab is three days from molting, and is placed in a pen where it is checked daily. Once the line has turned red the crab is two hours away from molting and is placed in another pen and checked hourly. Once the shell has been shed the crab is drowned and ready for the table.

Soft-shell crab stuffed with rice dressing, crab butter and grilled tasso;
served with rice dressing and asparagus

Shrimp

Native to the nearby Gulf of Mexico, the US's favorite shellfish is particularly popular in these parts and they will feature on just about every menu in Southern Louisiana. The ever-present shellfish appears in many forms from tiny gumbo shrimp to huge boiled Jumbos the size of a midget's bicep.

Shrimp can be boiled, cooked in a Cajun **shrimp étouffée** (shrimp smothered in gravy), fried in an overflowing **shrimp loaf** (poboy), or chilled in a **shrimp remoulade** (see the recipe in the Louisiana Gumbo Party chapter). Nearly every recipe that includes the generic term 'seafood' will include a portion of shrimp, from seafood gumbo to stuffed **mirliton** (vegetable squash).

Though many shrimp are now farmed due to constant demand, summer brings a treat from Gulf waters – native brown shrimp fresh from the nets. The warmer weather causes the shrimp to rise from the bottom of the deeper ocean and migrate towards the coast to breed. If they can avoid becoming victims of the watery food chain, they eventually end up in the fry pit or gumbo pot. The export of shrimp to other states and internationally is an important industry for Louisiana's coastal communities.

Crescent City Farmer's Market held every Saturday, New Orleans

Despite its familiar name, the signature New Orleans dish **barbecued shrimp** bears little resemblance to the slow-smoked meaty specialties of neighboring Texas. In this regionally popular seafood dish, there's no grill involved – the shrimp are pan-fried in their shells (heads on) with butter, olive oil, garlic, black pepper, Worcestershire sauce and other spices. It is utterly delicious, especially with lots of crusty French bread to soak up the sauce and a glass or two of crisp white wine to cut the near-overwhelming richness of the dish. Even in up-market establishments, it is not unusual to be given a paper bib to minimize splatter-related dry-cleaning bills.

Peeling shrimp at Uglesich's Restaurant, New Orleans

Oysters

These salty bivalves have always been abundant along the Gulf Coast – mounds of discarded shells litter ancient Native American sites as well as not-so-ancient picnic grounds alike – but in New Orleans, oysters, even in the simplest form, are considered high art. Restaurants across town are as likely to have on oyster bar as a liquor bar, and slurping these tender wonders on the half shell is the New Orleans pre- or between-meal tradition, with fabled fringe benefits as an aquatic aphrodisiac.

"Ersters," as they're called in the local Yat dialect, are farmed on the Gulf coast and are also taken from nearby rocks and reefs. Farmed oysters are available year round but are best in the colder months, when they're plump and salty. Oysters are most revered in New Orleans, where you can watch them being shucked – by the dozen or half-dozen – as you stand at one of the city's oyster bars (see Oyster Bars in the Where to Eat & Drink chapter).

Oysters also make their way into many Creole and Cajun specialties including **oyster soup** (a winter favorite), **oyster casserole**, gumbos and **rice dressing** (see Rice Dressing later in this chapter). They are also commonly coated in seasoned cornmeal and deep fried for a classic poboy filling.

More intricate treatments also abound in New Orleans restaurants, especially the old-line Creole establishments. The most famous local incarnation is in **Oysters Rockefeller** (named after John D because they're so rich) oysters baked on the shell along with a mixture of chopped spinach, bread crumbs, aromatic vegetables and warmed rock salt. Other fancy specialties include **Oysters Bienville** (with shrimp, mushrooms and wine sauce) and **Oysters Suzette** (with bacon, onion and bell pepper).

MONTHS WITH AN 'R' AND OTHER OYSTER DISCLAIMERS

Common-folk wisdom stipulates that you should only eat raw oysters in months that have an 'r' in them – exempting the hot months when the bivalves have a milky appearance. Despite the advent of modern farming, many locals still abide by this rule, and some oyster bars (like preternaturally clean Casamento's) shut down for much of the summer. Regardless of season, you're likely to see elaborately worded disclaimers on signs and menus of oyster bars. The most common warning reads as follows:

There may be a risk associated with consuming raw shellfish as is the case with other raw protein products. If you suffer from chronic illness of the liver, stomach, or blood, or have other immune disorders, you should eat these products fully cooked.

The lawyers have spoken. Now belly up for a 'dozen raw and a beer' and slurp away.

Freshly shucked oysters on the half shell

Crawfish

In Louisiana, the crawfish is everywhere. Throughout the region, you will see its bright red, beady-eyed visage staring at you from billboards and tourist brochures. Cartoon renditions of the sharp-clawed crustacean dance on souvenir T-shirts and festival posters. During springtime, restaurant and seafood market signs advertise Hot Boiled Crawfish, and the creature features on nearly every menu, from classy restaurants in the French Quarter to no-frills diners near the bayou.

Resembling tiny lobsters, crawfish grow wild in the freshwater wetlands of Louisiana and, through aquaculture (water farming), provide the state with a profitable industry. Elsewhere in the world, the crawfish goes by many other names, including *écrivesse* in France, yabby in Australia and crawdad or mudbug elsewhere in the States – but here in Louisiana, it's crawfish and *only* crawfish. Once considered a food of poverty and desperation, the crawfish is now a celebrated cornerstone of the state's diverse food culture. If you leave Louisiana without once tasting crawfish, you had better book a ticket back.

Crawfish can either be served fresh-boiled or in the form of pre-peeled tail meat. Being only a few inches in length, you need to eat a lot of crawfish to make a meal, and about 4-5lb (2-2½kg) of the little creatures per person is usual. When crawfish are in season – from early December to mid-July, but best from mid-February – the most popular way to enjoy them is boiled.

Crawfish boils, large-scale events that involve the boiling of hundreds of pounds of live crawfish, are a popular home-cooking tradition in Southern Louisiana. They are pleasantly chaotic outdoor affairs where crawfish are spilled onto newspaper-lined picnic tables and the assembled throng eats from the single pile of steaming crustaceans. If you don't get a chance to sit in on a crawfish boil, you can always try boiled crawfish at a no-nonsense seafood restaurant called a **boiling point** (see Boiling Points in the Where to Eat & Drink chapter). A meal of crawfish at a boiling point is a bit more controlled – servings are presented on aluminum beer trays – but it's a worthwhile experience nonetheless.

The tasty, well-armored creatures also form the basis for well-known Cajun dishes such as **crawfish étouffée** (crawfish smothered in gravy; see recipe), **crawfish boulettes** (fried stuffing balls), **crawfish jambalaya** (see Jambalaya later in this chapter) and the labor-intensive **crawfish bisque**. In this classic Cajun delicacy, boiled crawfish heads are filled with a sausage-like stuffing made of crawfish tails. They are then simmered in a rich roux-based crawfish soup, and served – like almost everything else in Louisiana – over white rice.

Crawfish Étouffée

Cajun cooks look for any excuse to serve an **étouffée** (literally, to smother; any dish slowly smothered in a rich gravy), and crawfish étouffée, made with the tender tail meat of the noble critter, is one of the most treasured dishes of the region. Nevertheless, you're just as likely to find shrimp or tougher cuts of beefsteak given a similarly delicious treatment. Commercially packaged crawfish tails (the most popularly exported form of crawfish) are perfect for this dish.

Ingredients

3½oz (100g)	butter	2 cups	onion, chopped
1 cup	bell peppers, chopped	1 cup	celery, chopped
1lb (500g)	peeled crawfish tails	1 tsp	salt
¼ tsp	cayenne	1 tbsp	flour
1 cup	water	3 tbsp	green onion, chopped
¼ cup	parsley, chopped		

Melt the butter in a large skillet or heavy-bottomed pot over medium heat. Add the onion and saute until soft and clear, about 10 minutes, then add the bell peppers and celery. Add the crawfish, salt and cayenne, and cook until completely mixed through.

Stir the flour into the water and add to the mixture. Bring to a slight boil. When the mixture thickens slightly, reduce heat to medium-low and simmer for 15-20 minutes, stirring occasionally. Add parsley and green onions. Stir for 5 minutes more. Serve immediately over white rice.

Makes 4 servings

Crawfish Farms

Crawfish have always flourished in Louisiana, but it was not until the 1960s that intensive crawfish farming began. Now 90% of the crawfish eaten in the US and half of that eaten in the rest of the world is farmed here.

Crawfish farming is carried out in large shallow ponds or increasingly in empty rice fields, providing local rice farmers with a lucrative secondary industry. Farmed crawfish are likely to find their way to a processing factory to be peeled and frozen, while the fruits of local waterways – advertised as Basin Crawfish on the signs of roadside vendors – are quickly cooked and brought bright-red to the table. Whatever their final destination, crawfish are caught in semi-submerged steel cages.

In many Acadian restaurants, diners will notice signs proclaiming No Chinese Crawfish, a local response to damaging market practices. By flooding the local market with cheaper tail meat, Chinese importers have earned the ire of local producers. Accusations of product dumping have attracted the attention of the Department of Commerce, which recently levied protective tariffs against the Chinese crawfish importers to protect local fishermen and their homegrown industry.

A Little Louisiana Legend

When the original Acadians were forced to leave Nova Scotia, the local lobsters (very loyal shellfish, indeed) decided to follow their adopted humans to Louisiana. During the arduous marathon swim, the hard-swimming crustaceans lost a lot of weight and most of their size. By the time the lobsters reached the bayous and swamps of Southern Louisiana to reunite with their beloved proto-Cajuns, they had transformed into the Acadiana's smaller, and now-totemic, crawfish.

Rocky and Lisa's Bayou Boudin & Cracklin Restaurant, Breaux Bridge

Pork

Pork has been on the menu here since the Europeans first traveled down the Mississippi. The first European exploratory party included 13 pigs (and then there were 12 ...). Of all the domesticated barnyard animals, the pig is perhaps the most noble and versatile. They grow quickly and are ready for slaughter in a shorter time than cattle, and because every part of the animal is used and pork has better preserving potential than beef, the pig is master of both the Louisiana and the Deep Southern meat domains. In Louisiana alone, the average annual pork consumption is 83lb (37kg) per adult. You will encounter pork and pork products in a variety of forms in Louisiana. Here are a few of the local specialties.

Ham

Considered the choicest cut of a pig, ham used to be a culinary expression of affluence. These days, you will find thick slices and a generous serving of it in your poboy; finely diced pieces in an eggplant stuffing; bigger chunks in your jambalaya; and juicy slices – known as ham steaks – on your plate as part of a country restaurant plate lunch or diner breakfast.

Chops & Roasts

These common cuts aren't exclusive to Louisiana, but here they're prepared with great reverence. Thick pork chops (usually on the bone) are either deep fried or smothered in onions and gravy. The loin roast can be dry cooked, stuffed with rice dressing or cooked slowly until fall-apart tender.

Andouille

Andouille (pronounced ahn-DOO-wee) is a spicy smoked pork sausage used as a flavoring ingredient in gumbos, jambalaya and other rice dishes. Andouille is noted for its peppery bite but the smoky flavor it imparts to dishes is its true value.

Gratons (Cracklins)

Gratons (called cracklins in the more Anglified area of the state) are made by cooking down pork skin until most of the fat is rendered and the skin itself is golden and crisp. Cut into small squares and seasoned with salt, spices and peppers, cracklins are a very popular snack throughout Cajun Louisiana. It can be added to cornbread to make cracklin bread.

Ponce (Chaudin)

This is a pig's stomach that has been stuffed with the same mixture used to make boudin, then smoked. The smoked ponce is then cooked, étouffée style, in a brown gravy.

Boudin

This Cajun specialty sausage is made with a mixture of pork, pork liver, green onions, green bell peppers, spices and cooked rice, piped into sausage casing. The most common version, **boudin blanc** (white boudin), is sold by the link in ready-to-eat form in groceries, meat markets and gas stations all over Acadiana. It's sometimes referred to as Cajun fast food and is eaten in Southern Louisiana as a breakfast or between-meal snack. To eat boudin, cut a link in half, insert an open end into your mouth, and slowly squeeze the filling out by the mouthful. Even though you can eat the elastic casing, it's considered questionable form.

Another rare variation, **boudin rouge** (red boudin) uses the blood of the freshly slaughtered pig. Boudin rouge can't be sold commercially due to health regulations governing the use of blood in products, but it is still made by families and some butchers on the side. If you meet the right people, your trip could be enriched with a sampling of the forbidden sausage (see Boucherie in the Celebrating with Food chapter and the boxed text Johnson's Grocery in the Shopping chapter).

Hog's Head Cheese

Traditionally this 'cheese' (actually formless gelatinous sausage) was made with the meat from the jowl of the pig, hence the name. You'll still find hog's head cheese made this way but you'll also find it made with cuts of pork that yield more meat. It is rich in fat and spices, and goes well on crisp crackers.

Tasso

Tasso is another highly prized butcher-shop specialty. It's basically a lean chunk of ham, cured with herbs and spices, **filé** (crushed sassafras leaves) and then smoked until it reaches the tough consistency of beef jerky. It is primarily used in small portions as a flavoring for soups, sauces and beans. Tasso is ridiculously hard to come by outside Louisiana so don't miss the chance to sample some.

Johnson's Grocery, Eunice

Spare Parts

The bits that are usually discarded elsewhere are used in inventive ways in the Deep South, and you can choose from pickled pigs' feet, **chitterlings** (tripe; also known as **chitlins**) or smoked ham hocks. Pigs' liver is often ground up for boudin.

Boudin and cracklins

CRACKLIN MAN

Rocky Sommelier is a man dedicated to the cause of cracklin. By 5 every morning except Monday he is in his flyscreen-walled kitchen on the banks of the Bayou Teche in Breaux Bridge.

With the sounds of the bayou coming to life in the early light, he begins. Rocky takes large pieces of pork skin and deftly slices them until he creates a small mountain of matchbox-sized pieces. He then ladles rendered pig fat saved from yesterday's cracklins into two black iron cauldrons. When the fat has reached the right temperature the pork skin pieces are added and cooked for 1½ hours. By this time it is getting mighty hot in the kitchen; the day is advancing and you begin to understand the necessity for starting so early.

Rocky and Lisa's Bayou Boudin & Cracklin Restaurant, Breaux Bridge

Once the pork skin pieces have cooked for the required time, Rocky quickly removes them from the hot fat. This fat is then used for cooking other treats (out in the cool room there are two turkeys waiting to be cooked), and some will be saved for starting the cracklins off tomorrow.

While the pork rinds are cooling, the heat of the fat is brought back up and the pieces are cooked again for another three minutes. Allowing the cooked pieces to cool slightly and plunging them back into very hot oil has the effect of sealing them and ensuring that they are crunchy.

The hot cracklins are removed from the oil, drained on newspaper, and seasoned with salt and cayenne pepper. Finally they are placed in large buckets, ready to be sold by the pound. By early afternoon all the cracklins will be sold, and Rocky rests up ahead of his next early start.

Rocky and Lisa's Bayou Boudin & Cracklin Restaurant, Breaux Bridge

Other Barnyard Meats
Chicken

Europeans brought fowl to the region and now it's as popular here as just about anywhere else in the developed world – even more so once you factor in Southern country-style fried chicken, and the chicken and sausage gumbo of the prairie Cajuns.

You can eat chicken stuffed, roasted, barbecued, stewed, fricasseed, and swimming with gooey dumplings. And don't even mention the chunks in your jambalaya and tender pieces in **sauce piquante** (spicy tomato-based stew). Chicken livers are also an essential ingredient in rice dressing (see the recipe later in this chapter).

Chicken and dumplings at Lea's Pies, Lecompte

Turkey

Turkey has made a jump from the Thanksgiving table guest of honor to become a more workaday dish. Meat markets around Lafayette (especially the famed Hebert's in Maurice) stuff the large fowl with a variety of flavorful fillings, including alligator-meat rice dressing and boudin stuffing. For a really fowl feast, look out for the **turducken** (a turkey stuffed with a chicken stuffed with a duck). Enterprising Cajun cooks have also put their crawfish boiling rigs to wintertime use by deep frying whole turkeys. The bones from the traditional American Thanksgiving bird are used to make turkey bone gumbo, a much revered seasonal specialty.

Beef

Only when the drier, treeless prairies of the central and northern areas of Louisiana were settled did raising cattle become a viable proposition. The semi-tropical climate wasn't ideal but cross-breeding local cows with brahmin varieties from India produced a breed that was heat and insect-tolerant. But even now much of the cattle raised is not for meat, and prodigious beef eaters are found mainly in the north of the region and the areas bordering Texas (see Northern Louisiana in the Regional Variations chapter).

Though not as popular as seafood or pork, beef does find its way into countless dishes in ground form – as in rice dressings, stuffed bell peppers, Creole-Italian meat sauces, and with the popular Northern Louisiana specialty, **Nachitoches meat pies** (see the recipe in the Regional Variations chapter). Younger milky veal is used in many more refined Creole dishes, such as tender veal scallops topped with mushrooms bordelaise.

Barbecue

Though there is some cross pollination from neighboring regions like east Texas and north Mississippi, barbecue isn't the spiritual issue that it is in other states. There are small joints in the city and countryside (such as Ms Heyster's in Mid-city New Orleans) where you can get the slow-smoked wonders, but the meaty treats are definitely more the exception than the rule. When you can get hold of good barbecue it can be anything from pork ribs to chicken to mutton and hot links, accompanied by soft white bread, coleslaw, potato salad, pinto beans, and plenty of beer or sweet soda. Dig in *mano a mano*, as true barbecue is a no-utensils affair.

Matilda's Country Kitchen, Eunice

STAPLES

Wild Game

The fertile wetlands and dense northern forests of Louisiana provide habitats for a wide variety of furred and feathered creatures. And, being an adaptive bunch, the inhabitants of the state have done their best to eat them all. Any time of year is hunting season for some animal or other, and what falls to the guns stocks the pots and fills the freezers of intrepid hunters and their families.

Rocky Mountain mixed grill, with blackened deer chop and buffalo tenderloin, Prajean's Restaurant, Lafayette

Considering that so much of the region is waterlogged, it's no surprise that duck is often on the menu. A duck and andouille gumbo, made with a dark roux and cooked over a campfire, is a culinary and cultural experience that's worth an early morning trip to the wintertime duck blinds. Flocks of migratory geese also have the misfortune of falling from Louisiana skies and into roasting pans. On the other side of the wild-bird scale, quail and dove can be fried, smothered, or stuffed with cornbread dressing loaded with ham and pecans.

And on land, deer shot in Louisiana coastal marshes or in neighboring states are 'processed' into versatile venison steaks, sausages, and the treasured backstrap (tender cut near the animal's spine). Smaller prey (including tasty rabbit) also end up smothered, roasted or stewed.

Roast duck with enoki mushrooms, roasted peppers and sherry sauce, Gamay Restaurant

THE BOLD PALATE

Louisiana natives (especially the Cajuns that live near the swamps and bayous) have a reputation for eating anything and everything that moves. The semi-tropical lands of Louisiana are home to a stunning array of wildlife, much of which is beautiful, plentiful, and delicious. Enterprising Native Americans and frontier-minded Cajuns weren't squeamish about catching, trapping and cooking animals that roam the swamps instead of the barnyard. Their diets were largely subsistence-based so anything that moved was fair game. To a certain extent, modern-day hunters keep the tradition alive (see Cajun Country in Regional Variations). Here are a few of the more high-profile foods that give the region this thoroughly omnivorous reputation.

Alligators

In the swamps and bayous of the Atchafalaya Basin, hunters often come across the American alligator (*Alligator mississippiensis*), Louisiana's most fearsome aquatic predator. These quick-swimming reptiles can grow up to 15 feet in length, but above the waterline, all that's visible are beady eyes and spinal ridges. During springtime, the mating bellows of male gators echo through the swamps, and on occasion, one of these sharp-toothed leviathans ends up in a Cajun trapper's dinner pot.

The American alligator was once hunted to the brink of extinction, and a ban on seasonal hunting was only lifted in 1982. Today, alligators are raised on farms specifically for their hides and meat.

Alligator meat is high in protein, low in fat and is best when taken from young animals. The meat is firm in texture and has a mild taste. The choicest cuts, and the ones you're most likely to find on restaurant menus, are the white tender tail meat and the fillets cut from along its backbone. Popular ways to serve alligator are in sausages, fried in strips or cooked in a flavorful **sauce piquante** (spicy tomato-based stew flavored with either cayenne or Tabasco sauce; recipe follows).

Frogs

When the French landed in Louisiana, they knew exactly what to do with these jumping amphibians. The bodies of these croaking critters aren't particularly meaty, when it comes to frogs, it's all about the legs. The only cut used from this plentiful amphibian is its tender, white leg meat that's most often battered and deep fried. Frog (like its swampland friend the alligator) is often described as tasting like chicken, and while the flesh does have a similar texture the meat has a subtle, nutty flavor all its own. The ones you eat in a restaurant will have been specially farmed, the bull frog being the most common.

STAPLES

Turtles

Thousand-year-old turtle shells have been found in ancient Native American rubbish dumps. Turtle meat from saltwater species (such as the leatherback, hawksbill and green sea turtles) and freshwater varieties (alligator snapping turtles) used to be eaten regularly, but its consumption is now limited to turtle soup. Farmed varieties are mostly used and alligator, veal or beef is increasingly substituted, as turtle meat becomes more difficult and expensive to procure. If you are ordering turtle soup, check with your wait-person that you are not getting 'mock' turtle. A good slug of sherry added at the table is the traditional accompaniment to turtle soup.

Alligator Sauce Piquante

Ingredients

1 tblsp	oil
1 tblsp	flour
1 lb (500g)	alligator tail meat, finely chopped
½	bell pepper, finely chopped
1	small onion, chopped
2 10oz (375g)	cans tomatoes
¼ cup	water
½ tsp	pepper sauce (or to taste)
	salt, pepper and cayenne pepper

In a large skillet, make a dark roux with the flour and oil (see Roux later in this chapter). Then add the alligator meat, bell pepper and onion, and cook until the vegetables are wilted.

Add the hot pepper, tomatoes and water, and season to taste with salt, pepper and cayenne. Cover and simmer for 1 hour. Serve over steamed rice.

Serves 8

Gumbo

In its broadest sense, gumbo is a spicy, full-bodied soup/stew traditionally served (like many French Louisiana specialties) over starchy steamed rice. The primary ingredients – which can include products from the sea, land, and air – vary from cook to cook and pot to pot.

For any Louisiana cook, gumbo is the personal interpretation of a classic process and their highly individualized culinary thumbprint. Close to the coast, you can find gumbos teeming with all manner of seafood (oysters, jumbo shrimp, half-shelled crabs) while prairie-bred Cajuns turn to their barnyard and smokehouse traditions for inspiration. Creole cooks in New Orleans often add tomato to their gumbos.

Seafood gumbo at The Frog City Cafe, Rayne

There are even seasonal variants that spring from other festive occasions, such as the Turkey Bone gumbo that follows the annual Thanksgiving feast. Successful hunters in Acadiana return with the raw ingredients necessary for a rich duck or wild goose version spiked with fat winter oysters. In short, a gumbo can be made with anything that's fresh and available.

The distinctively thick texture that separates gumbo from the broth-based soup family comes from the use of various thickening agents: dark roux, okra or the late addition of filé (FEE-lay; crushed sassafras leaves). Each technique has its adherents, with some cooks opting to use combinations of the three (roux *and* okra, filé *and* roux).

In most restaurants, gumbo is usually classified as a soup and is served as such on many menus. But in a larger practical sense, it's more of a one-pot meal and is always served with steamed long-grain white rice. One of the classic New Orleans meals comes from ordering a well-matched pair of smaller courses instead of a larger entree – a bowl of gumbo and half a poboy is always a winning combination (see the Gumbo recipe in the Louisiana Gumbo Party chapter).

STAPLES

CAJUN GUMBO TRADITIONS

The all-inclusive nature of gumbo makes it an all-purpose excuse for impromptu gatherings across Southern Louisiana. During the cooler months, a weekend is a typical trigger for family get-togethers.

Family members might gather around the stovetop to slowly stir the roux, trade stories and compare ingredient notes. What's in the gumbo this time? Chicken and andouille? Duck and oysters fresh from Abbeville? Some shrimp left over from last summer's fishing trip? Perhaps some of the duck that was bagged on a hunting trip. Just about anything can go into the pot for the long wintertime simmer.

Every gumbo seems to have a story associated with it, whether it's a tale of sharp shooting from a recent hunt, or a special shrimp and okra version that a beloved aunt made every Friday during her lifetime. Stories and tall tales always unfurl with a comforting bowl of steaming gumbo.

A common side dish in Cajun households is a creamy potato salad (made with homemade mayonnaise, of course) that begs the classic serving-time question, "Do you want your potato salad *on* your gumbo, or *in* your gumbo?" Newcomers might be most comfortable getting the soothing starch on the side, so it can be stirred in bite-by-bite according to taste and mood. After all, the beauty of this region-defining experience is in its variety, and you're sure to have a different gumbo (and more potato salad) next time. (See also the Louisiana Gumbo Party chapter and the boxed text A Bowl Full of History in the Culture chapter.)

WHEN LIGHT
IS FLASHING
STOP FOR
HOT BREAD

Bread

As you might expect from a Franco-centric culture, New Orleans is dependent on the joys of its daily bread, whether it be a hot loaf wrapped in restaurant linen or the foundation of the omnipresent poboy. The trademark bread of the Crescent City is an oblong French loaf with a crispy crust and feather-light interior. Where classic, thin Continental baguettes are mostly crust, the Louisiana French loaf has a soft, tender center – the better for sopping up sauces and soups.

Ironically, historians track today's bread to German settlers. While cornbread (or some version of cornmeal and water) was the original daily bread here, the majority of the European settlers preferred the wheat breads to which they were accustomed. While the wet soils of New Orleans could not support their cereal of choice, those who could afford it bought the wheat flour that came down the river from the midwestern farming communities.

Foodies Market, New Orleans

In the late 18th century, groups of German immigrants came to Louisiana and settled 25 miles up the river from New Orleans in Cote des Allemands (German coast). They chose the area because the drier land and fertile soil supported the cultivation of wheat. The Germans brought soft-kernel wheat seed with them. Soon wheat flour and many different types of European breads became readily available. The largest commercial bakery of European breads in the region is Leidenheimer's, which is still run by members of the fifth-generation German baking dynasty.

Bread-baking traditions are also strong in the small towns of Acadiana, where local bakeries flourish. At LeJeune's bakery in Jeanerette, a signal light flashes on the street as steaming loaves of bread emerge from the ovens. The canny locals bring sticks of butter for an on-the-spot treat.

Even the old school high-dollar restaurants in New Orleans encourage a hands-on relationship with bread. Warm, unsliced loaves arrive in the bread basket, and it's considered proper etiquette to tear the bread apart with your hands before slathering it with butter. Go ahead, make a mess – the restaurant staff expect it. (See also Cornbread later in this chapter.)

Wheat flour also goes into the making of roux, one of the foundations of Creole and Cajun cooking (see Roux later in this chapter).

Oyster poboy at Uglesich's Restaurant, New Orleans

The Poboy

Travelers may know this versatile specialty by one of its other names: submarine, grinder, or hoagie to name but a few. But make no mistake, New Orleans' poboy looms large in the city's food culture and transcends the meager classification of 'sandwich'.

Served on a soft yet crunchy loaf of local French bread, the poboy provides on-the-go sustenance and prevents hunger pangs in every corner of the state. Served everywhere from neighborhood groceries to interstate gas stations, poboys are the fast food of Louisiana.

The original poboys were hollowed-out loaves of French bread layered with cheap ingredients – potatoes and brown gravy – and served to the hungry New Orleans natives (striking workers, vagabonds, or other 'poor boys' depending on your choice of origin myth).

A word about scale – poboys are built to sustain hard-working people. They are usually sold by the whole or half, with half being a little more than what a normal person could comfortably eat in a single sitting.

In substance, the poboy is not very different from other large-format sandwiches, but their ready availability and near-infinite variety makes a poboy tour a quick way of tasting your way through the culinary pleasures of New Orleans. Once the poboy roll is sliced, all bets are off – you can stuff the bread with anything and everything that's edible and available.

Seafood variations include poboys stuffed with crispy fried shrimp and 'dressed' with a simple cast of condiments (mayonnaise, shredded iceberg lettuce and tomato slices). These densely packed seafood wonders are often referred to as **shrimp loaves** – a naming convention that also goes for fried oyster or catfish variations. During spring, poboy joints offer tender soft-shell crab sandwiches, a pricey but tasty seasonal specialty (see the boxed text Live Nude Crabs earlier in this chapter).

The same delicatessen tradition that gave birth to the muffuletta (see below) also provides more traditional lunchmeat combinations such as ham and cheese, turkey, and salami. The city's Italian presence hits the roll with meatballs and **red gravy** (spiced tomato sauce) or hot Italian sausage. Tender shreds of slow-cooked roast beef mixed with reduced beef gravy are the filling for the mostly-caramelized **debris** poboy. Whether filled with roast pork, fried crawfish, barbecued ham, or even french fries (a gravy-soaked nod to the original version), poboys represent Louisiana culinary culture crammed into a crunchy-soft roll.

The Muffuletta

It's only a slight exaggeration to say that New Orleans muffulettas are the size of manhole covers. In some cases, these sandwiches are actually *bigger*. Poboys may run on the large side, but the Italian cold-cut muffulettas are absolutely immense. Named for a round sesame-crusted loaf, muffulettas are layered with various selections from the local Sicilian deli tradition, including Genoa salami, shaved ham, mortadella and sliced provolone cheese.

But if it weren't for the signature spread – a salty, **olive salad** with pickled vegetables, herbs and plenty of garlic – the muffuletta would border on being a circular sesame-seed poboy. The olive salad – crunchy with marinated carrots, cauliflower and capers, and heavy on the olive oil – makes the New Orleans muffuletta a flavorful, greasy mess. The salad, a variation on Italian *giardiniera*, can differ in texture from chunky (as prepared by the original Central Grocery on Decatur Street) to finely minced (as served at Napoleon House on St Louis Street).

Muffulettas are a great option for frustrated vegetarians traveling in New Orleans, as they can easily be made without the inclusion of meat. The portion sizes are huge (a whole muffuletta is roughly equivalent to 2 whole poboys) and the oil content considerable (expect some oil to seep through the wrapper and bag). This behemoth of a sandwich is a true New Orleans masterpiece.

STAPLES

Rice

When a meal in French Louisiana doesn't come wrapped in a crunchy poboy roll, odds are that it's served on a bed of white rice. Many signature dishes from both the Creole and Cajun traditions are absolutely inseparable from the low-maintenance grain.

Whether you're digging into a tangy chicken **sauce piquante** (spicy tomato-based stew), an earthy boucherie **reintier de cochon** (pork backbone stew), or a traditional Monday helping of slow-cooked red beans (see Beans later in this chapter), the bowl or plate will start off with a healthy scoop of rice. The one constant of gumbo – be it seafood, poultry, or game – is the phrase 'serve over rice'.

Louisiana rice consumption is considerably higher than the rest of the nation, and even rivals that of some Asian countries. So strong is the local rice culture that in the 1970s, Japanese appliance companies successfully marketed automatic rice cookers to the home cooks of Southern Louisiana.

Bowls of slightly starchy, medium-grain rice are most common in Southern Louisiana, where rice fields dominate the marshy lands of the Cajun prairie. The texture is somewhere between glutinous Japanese sushi rice and the fluffier American long-grain varieties. The starchy texture helps the rice keep its integrity whether it's covered in a pool of shrimp étouffée or acting as sausage filler in links of hot Cajun **boudin** (see Boudin earlier in this chapter). Leftover rice is also commonly turned into a sweet and creamy rice pudding (see Rice Pudding later in this chapter). The drier, more discreet grains of long-grain rice are more common in dishes from the Anglo-influenced Soul Food traditions of Northern Louisiana, such as **hoppin' John** (rice and black-eyed peas).

Travelers seeking out zydeco clubs or bird sanctuaries west of Lafayette will encounter huge rice fields flooded with water. The town of Crowley celebrates its swampy harvest with the International Rice Festival in October.

From its humble beginnings, rice has grown into a significant industry. After the 1803 Louisiana Purchase transferred ownership of the state from France to the fledgling United States, American settlers from Georgia and Carolina explored the commercial possibilities of rice-growing in Southern Louisiana's damp terrain. While rice production in the other southern states faltered, Louisiana's surged ahead to become the third-largest producer in the US. Unlike the other rice-producing states, a large amount of the rice grown in Louisiana ends up on local tables, and is not exported.

The bayou town of New Iberia is home to the oldest operating rice mill in the US, the Conrad Rice Mill, which markets various products under the Konriko brand. Conrad also produces a famous Pecan Rice, a partially-hulled nut-flavored grain that's halfway between brown and white rice in texture.

Rice Dressing

It's a regional call whether you refer to this chicken, pork and rice melange as **rice dressing** (the traditional Cajun name) or **dirty rice** (a Deep Southern slang variant). Either way, it's a tasty way to use the giblets (livers and gizzards) from a roast chicken or holiday turkey, and any leftover rice.

Rice Dressing

Ingredients

1	large onion, finely chopped
3	celery stalks, finely chopped
1	green bell pepper, finely chopped
2 cloves	garlic, minced
2 tblsp	vegetable oil or butter
12oz (375g)	chicken livers, chopped
1lb (500g)	ground beef or pork
1 pint (500ml)	beef stock
4 cups	cooked long-grain rice
¹/₂ cup	chopped green onions
1 tsp	cayenne pepper
¹/₂ tsp	dried or fresh thyme
	salt and black pepper to taste

In a heavy-based frying pan saute the onion, celery, bell pepper and garlic in the butter or oil until soft. Add the livers, beef or pork, and stock, cook for 3 minutes. Add the rice and cook until the liquid is absorbed. Add the green onions and season to taste with salt, black pepper, cayenne pepper and thyme. Mix well.

Serves 6

Jambalaya

Hearty, rice-based jambalaya (johm-buh-LIE-uh) is a Louisiana classic. It is loosely based on Spain's *paella*, although in practical terms it's probably closer to *arroz con pollo* (chicken and rice). Jambalaya can include just about any combination of fowl, shellfish or meat, but usually includes ham, hence the dish's name (ham in Spanish is *jamon*). The meaty ingredients are sauteed with onions, bell pepper, and celery, and cooked with raw rice and water into a flavorful mix of textures.

Jambalaya is a flexible workaday dish that carries with it an added level of informality, as it is less susceptible to culinary purism and caters well to

Annie's Chicken & Sausage Jambalaya

Ingredients

1	chicken cut into frying pieces (with our without skin) or substitute a few chicken breasts (whole or boned)
5 tblsp	vegetable oil
2	large onions (about baseball size) cut into medium rings
4 tblsp	vegetable oil
1lb (500g)	smoked sausage (andouille, kilbasa, or other variety cut crosswise into ¼ inch disks)
1	large onion, diced
1	medium bell pepper, diced
1	rib celery, diced
2 cloves	garlic, minced
2 cups	uncooked rice
½ cup	chopped green onion
	all-purpose Cajun seasoning

Heat the oil in the heaviest pan you can get (cast-iron Dutch oven with a snug-fitting lid preferred). Sprinkle the chicken pieces with Cajun seasoning. When the oil starts to smoke, place pieces in pan and let them cook until thoroughly browned. Remove the chicken from the pan and add the onion rings. Before long, the onions should start to sweat. Stir constantly, gently scraping the bottom of the pan to dislodge the browned chicken bits. Continue to cook the onions until they become soft and golden, then turn the heat down and slowly cook about 5 more minutes. After the onions are pretty wilty, return the chicken and cook for 45 minutes, uncovered, adding a little water if needed (note: more water, more gravy).

In another heavy pan, heat oil and saute the sausage until browned. Add the onion, pepper, celery and garlic. Cook until the vegetables wilt and turn slightly brown. Add this mixture to the chicken.

Stir in the rice and add 3 cups of water. (if your pan is small, make sure to compensate for rice swelling. You should have just a little room left in the pan above the rice/water level.) Season to taste with Cajun seasoning, cover it, and lower the heat to simmer. Resist the urge to open the pot for about 20 minutes while the rice cooks. After this time, check the rice for doneness. If it's still crunchy, add a little water and cover for another few minutes. When the rice is tender, stir in the chopped green onions, adjust the spices and enjoy.

Louisiana kitchen improvisation. Whatever's on hand can always fit into a jambalaya. There are, however, some stylistic differences between city and country jambalayas – New Orleans Creole versions are more likely to incorporate tomatoes into the mix, but you can also find Cajun cooks that add the tangy fruit to their versions (even though they'd *never* add it to their gumbo).

Jambalaya is also an excuse for large-scale outdoor cookery, with huge cast-iron pots bubbling over butane-powered crawfish burners. Any local music, food or culture festival will feature jambalaya as a low-maintenance, high-flavor 'festival food' (see the Celebrating with Food chapter).

COOKING UP A STORM

The best advertisement that jambalaya ever got was from country-and-western singer Hank Williams. While playing juke joints in Northern Louisiana in the 1940s, Williams Senior (the only *real* Hank) – took the traditional Cajun song *Grand Texas* and wrote a catchy two-chord tribute to Cajun country called *Jambalaya*.

Jamba-liiiiiiiiiiii, Crawfish piiiiiiiiiiiie, fee-lay gumbo
For tonight I'm a gonna see my cher uh mee o
Pick guitar, fill fruit jar and be gay-o
Son of a gun, we'll have big fun on the bayou.

His ditty became a nationwide hit and, sadly, has been adopted by questionable international lounge bands and karaoke crooners ever since.

Ingredients for jambalaya

Beans

Wherever you find rice, you'll find beans to go on top. As an inexpensive and low-maintenance source of protein, beans have played an integral role in the culinary history of New Orleans, as well as in the rest of Louisiana.

Red Beans (& Rice)

The combination of red beans and rice is a lunch tradition synonymous with Mondays throughout the state, but especially in New Orleans. Before the advent of modern appliances, Monday was traditionally wash day, and in a world before white goods, it took all day to hand-wash the family laundry. So a pot of red beans would go on the stove along with the ham bone left over from Sunday dinner, and the longer it cooked, the better it tasted. By the time the washing was finished, supper was ready.

In the absence of red beans, larger maroon kidney beans are often substituted. The flavoring meat can also be spicy **andouille** sausage or chunks of pork **tasso**, a long-smoked Cajun specialty (see the Pork section earlier).

Black-Eyed Peas

This hearty bean is especially popular where Soul Food dominates. Also called purple-hull peas for their colorful pod, they are creamy beige with a single dark spot (eye) near the center. Black-eyed peas are traditionally cooked with a flavoring meat (ham hocks and salt pork are common) and eaten on New Year's Day for luck (see the Celebrating with Food chapter). Vinegar-based **sport pepper sauce** (see Louisiana Pepper Sauce later in this chapter) or sliced jalapeno peppers are often used to spice up black-eyed peas.

Green Beans

The home gardens of Louisiana produce more than their fair share of this tender springtime specialty. Menus see these thin green wonders alternately as snap beans or string beans and are generally prepared with a healthy dose of flavoring pork. Green beans are also often smothered together with small, red new potatoes for a filling vegetable course.

Other Beans

Other variations on the beans and rice combo have worked their way into Louisiana food lore. Stewed white (or navy) beans are cooked as you would red beans and served with crispy fried catfish or tender roast pork. Tender, pale green butter beans (also called lima beans) are a mainstay of country restaurant menus. These creamy-textured legumes combine with kernels of sweet corn to make **succotash** (suffering or no). Sicilian immigrants to New Orleans brought along their sacred fava beans, which are prepared to celebrate the Feast Day of St. Joseph (see the Celebrating with Food Chapter).

Red Beans & Rice (Vegetarian Dance Remix)

This classic Cajun standby provides a good launching point for learning about the three basic peppers (black, white and red), as well as the power of the Louisiana Holy Trinity (onions, bell pepper and celery).

Ingredients

1lb (500g)	dried red or kidney beans (soaked in water for at least 4 hours)
4 cloves	fresh garlic, finely chopped
2	medium onions, finely chopped
2	medium bell peppers, chopped
3	ribs celery, finely chopped
4 tblsp	olive oil

Herbs & spices

2	bay leaves	1 tsp	black pepper
1/2 tsp	white pepper	1/4 tsp	red pepper
2 tsp	dried basil	3/4 tsp	rubbed sage
4 tblsp	dried parsley	1 bunch	green onions, chopped
2 tsp	salt (then to taste)		

Saute the garlic and onion in the olive oil until the onions get lazy (limp and transparent). Add the celery and bell pepper and saute for 5 minutes. Pour the soaked beans and water into the mix, then simmer until beans soften (1-2 hours). (You can also use canned beans to save time, but if you do, cut back on the added salt.) Add the peppers and dried herbs, tailoring the spice to your own liking.

Remove one cup of the beans, mash them with a fork in a bowl then return to the pot. This will add a creamy texture to the final product. Add the parsley and green onions. Simmer for 15 minutes, fine-tune the spices and serve over rice.

Serves 8

Corn

Corn was one of the first foods introduced to European settlers by the Native Americans, and now ranks as one of the keystone staples of American cuisine. While the settlers preferred wheat flour, the cereal didn't grow well in Louisiana's moist lowlands so it was only available when it came down the river from Illinois. They were soon turning the plentiful corn into a variety of breads and other dishes.

Corn is no longer grown as a significant commercial crop here but remains an important staple. It is enjoyed at home simply buttered or as part of a seafood boil (see Boiling Points in the Where to Eat & Drink chapter). Roasted corn on the cob is a popular treat at fairs and festivals.

Papa's Cornbread

This is a recipe learned at the stove of Achille Leon Hebert, longtime Baton Rouge attorney and the author's grandfather. It's a classic grainy cornbread (not too sweet) with buttermilk for a little bit of tang.

Ingredients

1 cup	cornmeal
2 tblsp	flour
2 tblsp	baking powder
½ tblsp	salt
1 tblsp	sugar
1 cup	buttermilk
1	large egg
3-4 tblsp	vegetable oil (or bacon grease)

Preheat the oven to 425°F (225°C). In a large bowl, sift together the cornmeal, flour, baking powder, sugar and salt. Mix in the egg and buttermilk.

In a small cast-iron skillet, heat up the oil until it starts smoking. Swirl the oil around to coat the inside of the skillet. Then pour the hot oil into the batter and mix vigorously until the oil is well blended. Bake for 25 minutes or until slightly brown on top.

If you like your cornbread brown on both sides, take the skillet out at 20 minutes and carefully flip the bread without breaking it (running a knife around the edge helps).

Serves 4

Fresh corn is also the major component of a popular Cajun dish called **maque choux**, which is made from fresh corn kernels, bell peppers (or onions) and tomatoes. Maque choux is believed to have been an original Native American dish, which was taught to the Cajuns.

Dried corn is ground into a coarse meal that is used in cooking throughout the region. It's used to dredge seafood (especially oysters and catfish) before deep frying for a flavorful, crispy crust.

Grits & Hominy

Historically, corn kernels were tenderized by soaking them in lye and water to remove the tough outer skins. These skinned kernels were dried and became hominy, an important food to the Native Americans as it could be stored for long periods. Once corn had been turned into hominy, it could then be ground into a coarse white meal known as grits.

Grits are prepared as a porridge (similar in texture to polenta) and are served as a common side option at any Northern Louisiana diner breakfast. Since they register on the bland end of the flavor spectrum, they're best 'enhanced' with plenty of butter, black pepper and hot sauce. Grits are also served in the classic New Orleans brunch dish **grillades and grits** (grilled beef or veal slices braised in tomato sauce and served with hominy).

Cornbread

Cornbread is the simple, everyday bread most often seen on Southern country-style and Soul Food menus. Leavened by baking soda and baking powder instead of yeast, this simple batter bread can be whipped up in minutes and cooked on campfire or stovetop as easily as an oven. Oven or no, cornbread is best cooked in a cast-iron skillet (see Special Utensils in the Home Cooking & Traditions chapter).

In its simplest forms, ground cornmeal is mixed with water and a little salt and cooked as **hoe cakes** or **Johnny cakes** (cooked on a hot piece of metal); **ash cakes** (cooked in the fire) or **corn pone** (cooked in an oven). More common variations use wheat flour, bacon grease, eggs and buttermilk for flavor and a lighter texture.

There are many variations that you can expect to find in home and restaurant bread baskets, including muffins, **corn sticks** (cornbread baked in corn-shaped moulds), **cracklin bread** (cornbread with cracklins added) and **hush puppies** (balls of deep-fried cornbread batter). Crumbled cornbread is mixed with different combinations of ham, pecans, herbs, sausage or shrimp and served as a stuffing for poultry. Leftover cornbread is often eaten soaked in milk for breakfast. The Cajun variation of this morning meal, which involves cooking cornbread batter until crispy before serving with milk and cane syrup, is called **coush coush** (KOOSH-koosh).

Herbs, Spices & Seasonings

Though many people directly associate the spicy flavors of Louisiana cooking with fiery cayenne pepper, the culinary emphasis in both Cajun and Creole foods is on strong yet balanced flavors.

The trademark herbs and spices of Louisiana cooking show how the state's culinary traditions melded the bold flavors from European traditions and mixed them with indigenous ingredients (filé, bay leaves) to form a culinary synthesis.

THE THREE PEPPERS

Varying combinations of these three peppers are responsible for giving Louisiana food its distinctive spiciness. These peppers are also the primary components of now-common **Cajun seasoning** mixes (see Spice Mixes later in this chapter).

Cayenne pepper
Cayenne pepper, a powdered version of a native Louisiana hot pepper, is the most visible (and as such, overused) pepper in the Louisiana repertoire. Due largely to the Cajun Hot fad of the 1980s, cooks throughout the US routinely shovel toxic levels of cayenne into *any* dish and affix the adjective 'Cajun' to it. Cajun cheeseburgers. Cajun popcorn. Cajun-style New England baked clams. If you've ever burned your throat on a faux-Cajun dish, you've been hit with a cayenne overdose.

Cayenne pepper provides afterburn (lingering heat that registers toward the back of the palate and throat) and as such, should be treated with respect and restraint. Home cooks would be well advised to add cayenne with a light touch, preferably splitting the specified amount in thirds and adding the powerful dust gradually, tasting after each addition to see when you've hit your limit.

Black pepper
Ground from a peppercorn, this common tabletop spice plays a crucial role in Louisiana cuisine by providing peppery spice in the front of the mouth. In the home kitchen, freshly ground black pepper can give the most mundane dishes an amazing depth of taste, especially when compared to the common pre-ground spice.

White Pepper
The third member of the essential pepper trio, this milder peppercorn fills the taste hole between black and cayenne pepper by affecting the middle of the mouth's upper palate. Made from riper 'berries' than its black counterpart, white pepper is the 'mystery spice' in many seasoning mixes. You may not be able to identify it by flavor, but you'll know when it's missing.

STAPLES

Chiles, for Tabasco sauce, Avery Island

ROUX

It's been said that every Cajun recipe (and many a Creole soup and sauce) starts with the five-word phrase, "first, you make a roux," and with good reason. The classic concoction gives the Cajun dishes their characteristic richness and deep, nutty flavor. The recipe for roux hails from the French kitchen and is the primary thickener and flavoring agent in gumbos, étoufées, and other Acadian standbys.

Being able 'to roux' is a fundamental skill in the Louisiana cooking repertoire – once you get the hang of making a deep brown roux, you're exactly halfway to perfection. The availability of ready-made roux mixes have brought convenience to this time-consuming process. Such products are a good shortcut for beginners, but there's a certain joy to making a roux from scratch and learning this important skill.

When picking a shade of roux, many cooks follow this rule: the darker the meat, the lighter the roux. This means chicken gumbo calls for a dark roux while heartier game meats (such as venison) call for a lighter roux.

Some cooks swear by an extremely dark roux for their dishes, but the novice should be extremely careful when attempting the darker shades. It doesn't take much to burn the mixture, and once black bits start appearing in the roux, it's all over. The culprit is usually impatience and high flame. When this happens, clean out the pot, pop open another beer and start again (on low this time).

Roux

Ingredients

1	heavy-bottomed cast-iron skillet or pot	1 cup	neutral-flavored oil (vegetable, canola, whatever)
1 cup	all-purpose flour	1	wooden spoon
1	cooking companion		no watches or clocks

The process couldn't be simpler, you just stand around a heavy pot with a wooden spoon, a low fire, and maybe a cold beer. Stand, stir, and sip. Talk to your cooking partner about pressing matters of the day or great meals past. Keep stirring. Do not, under *any* circumstances, look at a clock. As long as you're on Roux Patrol, keep time by the color of the mixture. The longer you stir, the darker it gets. The most-used types are: **blonde**, a delicate-tasting roux that looks like thin peanut butter, used for darker, more full-flavored meats (especially wild game); **medium**, a good beginner's roux. The color has been described as "the color of an Indian's behind" by an old Cajun woman; and **chocolate**, could it get more self-explanatory? Shoot for about a shade lighter than chocolate syrup.

Spice Mixes & Cajun Seasoning

Rather than constantly mixing together individual spices, Cajun cooks keep their favorite spices pre-mixed and ready to use at a moment's notice. Usually a blend of salt, the three peppers, spices (such as paprika or granulated garlic) and dried herbs, these mixes can be purchased commercially (Tony Chachere's and Konriko are both standard brands), acquired from local meat markets, or created at home. Many different mixes are marketed as **Cajun seasoning**, but buyer beware, as some companies go heavy with cayenne at the expense of a balanced flavor.

Bay leaf

The aromatic leaf of the bay laurel tree bound Native Americans and settling Europeans together culinarily. It was already in common use among the Native Americans, and for the Europeans – particularly the French – the bay leaf was a gastronomic gem. Whole bay leaves are used to flavor many savory dishes, particularly long-cooked beans.

Louisiana Pepper Sauce

One local use for the hot pepper (a successful transplant from elsewhere in the Americas) is in the vinegar-based hot sauces that are offered as standard seasoning in Louisiana restaurants. A bottle of the local hot sauce will often be placed on every table along with salt and pepper shakers.

Usually a fermented mix of pepper pods, salt and vinegar, pepper sauces have departed from the standard red-pepper variety in recent years. The ubiquitous Tabasco Sauce, produced by Avery Island's McIlhenny dynasty, has recently expanded its line to include other peppery bases such as green jalapeno, mild garlic, and the painful habanero.

Louisiana pepper sauces are also popular among the booming subculture of pepper-obsessed chile-heads in the US and abroad. The boom in Louisiana specialty foods has resulted in a peppery renaissance of epic proportions. Small companies and home-based businesses in Louisiana are churning out palate-scorching concoctions with names such as Mean Devil Woman Cajun Hot Sauce, Popie's Hotter'n Hell Sauce and VampFire Hot Sauce. **Sport peppers**, yellow peppers steeped in vinegar, are a common seasoning for Soul Food dishes like stewed greens or black-eyed peas.

Parsley & Green Onions

These twin greens are important finishing herbs in the Cajun tradition. Usually minced and added at the last stage of cooking, parsley and green onion (also known as scallions or onion tops) provide a distinctively 'green' flavor to gumbos, jambalayas, and other classic dishes. Green onions are also used to spice the better boudin in Southern Louisiana.

SASSAFRAS & FILÉ

Native Americans were the first to use filé, made from the ground leaves of the sassafras tree (*Sassafras altltidum*) to thicken and season their food. Then they let the French in on their secret. Filé powder is now integral to Creole cooking, where it's used to thicken and flavor gumbo and other dishes.

The roots of the tree were also used to make a tea that the Native Americans took as a general tonic and as an aid to lowering blood pressure. The tea made from the roots is the basis of root beer (see Root Beer in the Drinks chapter). Sassafras roots contain an active ingredient called safrole that makes the root hallucinogenic and carcinogenic if consumed in large quantities.

Sassafras leaves and filé

Creole mustard

Somewhere between the sauce and spice categories, there lies Creole mustard. More rustic and flavorful than its yellow American counterpart, brownish Creole mustard is similar to a European whole-grain mustard except that the mustard seeds are marinated in vinegar during preparation. Zatarain's is the standard brand throughout the state. It's vital ingredient in **shrimp remoulade** (see the recipe in the Louisiana Gumbo Party chapter).

Horseradish

Tiny jars of prepared horseradish can be spotted at any oyster bar or outdoor boiling event. This powerful paste provides a distinctive sinus-clearing heat to the 'mix yourself' cocktail sauce that accompanies raw oysters or boiled crawfish. Approach with caution.

Seafood boil

Also known as **crab and shrimp boil**, this ubiquitous commercial mixture can be found just about anywhere seafood is dipped into boiling water. A **boiling bag** (a kind of industrial *bouquet garni*) can contain a blend of bay leaves, mustard seeds, cayenne pepper, peppercorns, cloves and allspice – the last two having come from the West Indies. There are many different commercial crab boil mixes available, and each varies in its composition. Seafood boil also comes in powdered or highly concentrated liquid form.

TABASCO – AVERY ISLAND

Harvesting chiles at the Tabasco plant

STAPLES

Avery Island in Southern Louisiana is home to the most recognized brand of hot sauce in the world, Tabasco. Just a few drops of this potent concoction can resuscitate even the blandest meal.

According to the Tabasco legend, Edward McIlhenny was given the seeds for some peppers (*Capsicum frutescens*) by a soldier returning through Louisiana from the Mexican War. McIlhenny planted them in his garden on Avery Island where they flourished.

During the Civil War the island was raided by the Union troops, who were after salt from the salt mine. Before taking their leave, the troops destroyed the house and garden. The only surviving plants were the hot pepper bushes. McIlhenny tooled around in the kitchen with these peppers and Tabasco was born. He persuaded some friends to sell it and an empire was launched.

Harvesting chiles at the Tabasco plant

Another story tells of Maunsel White, a man who lived in New Orleans some years before McIlhenny 'invented' Tabasco. White was selling a hot sauce he had invented, Maunsel White's Tabasco Pepper Sauce, but had neglected to patent his creation. McIlhenny wisely did so.

Patenting aside, the West Indians have been making sauces with hot peppers for some time, and it's possible that the idea for pepper sauce made its way to the Deep South from the West Indies.

Many years after patenting the sauce, the McIlhenny family set about trademarking the Tabasco name. Courts throughout the US dismissed the case, given that Tabasco is the name of a Mexican province and also the

Pepper sauce mix

A scoop from a barrel of pepper sauce mash

Barrels of pepper sauce

Harvesting chiles at the Tabasco plant, Avery Island

Packing the pepper sauce

name of a hot pepper. However, the Louisiana court granted the McIlhenny family the exclusive rights to say "made from Tabasco peppers" and to call a sauce made from Tabasco peppers "Tabasco Sauce". So any other sauce made with Tabasco peppers, but not made by the McIlhenny family, cannot call itself Tabasco sauce or say that it was made from Tabasco peppers. All these other sauces are usually labeled 'hot sauce' or 'pepper sauce'.

Tabasco is sold worldwide and its label is printed in 15 languages – a testament to patenting, trademarking and friends in the right places.

Perhaps the best known of the hot sauces used in Cajun or Creole cooking

Sauces

With Louisiana's strong French roots, it's no surprise that many of its trademark dishes are based on sauces, from the simple to the complex. Look for the more sophisticated variants on New Orleans' many Creole menus.

Remoulade Sauce

This is a spicy sauce that differs widely from the French mayonnaise based classic. Many New Orleans recipes for this sauce use a base of tomato ketchup spiked with horseradish, red pepper, and Creole mustard. Most often found on chilled shrimp as **shrimp remoulade** (see the recipe in the Louisiana Gumbo Party chapter).

Mayonnaise

Mayonnaise in Louisiana is considered a relative to the French original rather than a bland white sandwich spread. In many homes and restaurants, you'll find a pale yellow version of this continental classic on salads or in dishes such as coleslaw or potato salad.

Hollandaise Sauce

This rich egg-and-butter sauce is an important ingredient in more upscale brunch offerings, such as eggs benedict, eggs sardou and trout margeury. **Béarnaise Sauce** is a common variant on hollandaise that includes a mixture of herbs, shallots and vinegar.

Cocktail Sauce

A regular at oyster bars and crawfish boils. Mix your own cocktail sauce with ketchup, prepared horseradish, pepper sauce and lemon.

Some of the ingredients that are essential in Cajun or Creole cooking

STAPLES

Vegetables

With its long growing season and rich bottom-land soil, the land around New Orleans provides a wide range of farm fresh vegetables. Whether they're brought in for sale at the French Market or purchased from roadside vendors, the products of Louisiana gardens are an essential part of the local culinary tradition.

THE HOLY TRINITY

The combination of three aromatic vegetables – white onion, sweet green bell pepper, and celery – is popular enough in Cajun and Creole cooking to warrant the highly Catholic nickname, The Holy Trinity. Classic local dishes such as gumbo, red beans, courtboullion and sauce piquante all require that this flavorful trio be sauteed in the initial stages of the cooking process. Their collective importance is similar to the *mirepoix* (base of onion, celery and carrot) in continental French cuisine. In many dishes, garlic is also added, but that messes up the Biblical metaphor. The sweet bell pepper sometimes goes it alone as a dinner course, filled with meat and bread stuffing.

The home-grown **Creole tomato** is revered in Louisiana as a true wonder of nature, and cooks integrate it into a wide variety of dishes. Creole cooks are likely to add the flavorful fruit to their gumbo and jambalaya recipes. Cajuns in the kitchen are likely to smother okra or summer squash with a tomato or two. But at peak tomato season, the traditional preparation is to serve the fresh-picked beauties as the simplest of salads – sliced thick with a sprinkle of salt and, if you're feeling decadent, a generous dollop of home-made mayonnaise.

Seeking out tomatoes at local truck stands is a popular activity during the long, hot Louisiana summer (see Truck Stands in the Shopping chapter). Popular varieties aside from the supernaturally tangy and flavorsome Creole tomatoes, include blood tomatoes (named for their color and juiciness) and large bright beefsteak tomatoes.

Immature hibiscus bud **okra** came with the African slaves and has made a distinct culinary impression on the Deep South as a whole. Okra has a significant amount of mucilage (also known as goo) and is used as a primary thickener in some gumbo recipes (see Gumbo earlier in this chapter and the recipe in the Louisiana Gumbo Party chapter). It can also be served as crispy pickled pods or breaded and deep fried until crunchy.

Significant native vegetables include the large number of varieties of squash that choke the markets during the summer season. Hefty yellow squash and huge zucchini (courgettes) show up on many a diner menu in fried or smothered form. No matter which variety is used, squash (and many other vegetables) will usually be cooked long and soft, as opposed to quick and crisp.

A native variety of sweet potato is known here as **Louisiana yam**. Yams, which are also widely available, arrived with the African slaves and soon became a cornerstone of local cuisine. Nevertheless if you see yams on a menu, you can safely assume it is actually sweet potato. Candied yams are a popular side dish served with roasted meats, but Cajuns are fond of baking the tuber until tender and eating it with plenty of sweet butter.

Turnip, mustard and collard greens – individually or in combination – are Soul Food regulars. Nothing fancy going on here – greens are usually cooked with a chunk of flavoring meat, sprinkled with a bit of pepper sauce, and served with cornbread. The flavorful cooking broth is known as **pot liquor**.

Purple **eggplants** (aubergines) sprout up in gardens across the state and end up on plates smothered with local tomatoes or stuffed with seafood and baked. Italian cooks in the city are also likely to transform the hefty vegetable into eggplant *parmigiana*, which is cooked with **red gravy** (spiced tomato sauce). Similar preparations await the **mirliton**, a vegetable squash that is is eaten throughout Latin America and Asia, where it is known as chayote.

And let's not forget the humble potato, which shows up in standard American – and not so familiar – forms. In old-line New Orleans restaurants, you're likely to see stylistically French preparations of the potato, including **Lyonnaise** (sauteed with onion), **au gratin** (casserole baked with cream sauce and cheese) and **brabant potatoes** (cubed, deep fried and drizzled with butter).

French Market, New Orleans

STAPLES

Fruit

You can buy a huge variety of fruit in markets these days, although much of it is shipped in from elsewhere. There is, however, some produce that is grown locally and plays an important role in shaping the local diet.

Fruit stall owned and operated by three generations of the one family, New Orleans

Strawberries

Or as the signs proudly state, Ponchatoula Strawberries. The local berry-growing area of the same name (northwest of New Orleans) produces fruits that are simultaneously tangy and sweet. When these Louisiana beauties hit the markets in late spring and summer, it's the perfect time for strawberry shortcake, tangy strawberry pies, and homemade strawberry preserves. Fresh sliced berries on hand-cranked homemade ice cream also ranks as a gift from the summertime gods.

Dewberries

Also known as wild blackberries, these sweet/tart berries grow in sticky brambles along roadsides and fencerows throughout the state. When the summer berries turn deep purple, intrepid pickers hit the bushes, braving sharp thorns and snakebite for a bucketload. Along with being eaten fresh they fill many of the region's delicious **cobblers** (single-crust deep dish pies) and jams, and sometimes form the basis for wine (see Wine in the Drinks chapter). Blueberries and huckleberries are also widely popular.

Peaches

Another roadside sign to look for is one advertising Ruston Peaches, a popular summer fruit eaten fresh or baked into dessert pies. The sweet, blushing freestone fruit is also turned into cooling ice cream, perfect for the southern summers.

Other Fruits

Watermelons grow well in the semi-tropical conditions and are commonly purchased from roadside truck stands during summer (see Truck Stands in the Shopping chapter). These huge green-striped melons grow just about everywhere, and the towns of Franklinton (near New Orleans) and Farmerville (in Northern Louisiana) have competing festivals in honor of the sweet crop.

Oranges came from the West Indies and are now an important commercial crop. The area south of New Orleans around Port Sulphur is the chief orange-growing district and the Washington orange is its specialty. Trees filled with easy-peeling **satsumas** (mandarin oranges) are common throughout Southern Louisiana.

Figs, brought by the French, are often preserved and used as pie fillings as well as adding a special touch to glazes and sauces for duck and poultry. The crabapple-like fruit of Northern Louisiana's **mayhaw** tree makes wonderfully tangy jelly that's common to the Arkansas borderlands. **Muscadine**, also known as **scupperdongs** or **fox grapes**, are most commonly used for wine making (see Wine in the Drinks chapter). You will also find them made into jellies and used in sauces to pair with roast meat.

Muscadine grapes from the Old South Winery, Natchez, Mississippi

Pecans

Though the peanut rules many other southern states, the pecan is Louisiana's nut of choice. These nuts are indigenous to the region and were often used in cooking by the Native Americans. They also extracted oil from these versatile nuts. Pecan trees grow well in the Deep South and, while driving the back roads in the north of the region, you will see deep shady groves of these huge trees. Pecans are used mostly in sweet dishes and are a common ingredient is stuffing for poultry and vegetables. Pecan pralines (pronounced PRAW-leens in Louisiana) are an extremely popular sweet treat (see the recipe in the Louisiana Gumbo Party chapter).

Pecan pie at Lea's Pies, Lecompte

Making pecan pralines, New Orleans

Sugarcane

Sugarcane was introduced as a commercial crop by the Spanish when they gained control of the territory in 1762. It is now the second largest cash crop in Louisiana, which also has the highest consumption of cane sugar per head in the nation.

In the late 1700s, sugar was in high demand as a luxury item and the fortunes of many plantation owners were built on the sweet crop. Much of it was grown with slave labor and after the Civil War – and the abolition of slavery – the industry fell on hard times. It has now restabilized itself after a series of boom/bust cycles and the process is fully mechanized and popular in the bayou country around New Iberia.

Before the advent of strong-stalk hybrids, children could peel and chew on the cane's bamboo-like stalks to get at the sweet, flavorful juice stored in the fiber. But more weather resistant breeds make this practice increasingly rare.

Cane syrup, a sweet specialty of Abbeville, is made by boiling down the pressed sugarcane juice in cast-iron pots until it thickens. The resulting syrup, a sweeter version of molasses, is popularly poured over hot biscuits or **pain perdu** (literally, lost bread, a variation of skillet-fried French bread) for breakfast. It's also a key ingredient in **gateau de sirop**, a traditional spiced cake associated with Southern Louisiana.

STAPLES

Harvesting sugarcane

Desserts

The end of a meal anywhere in Louisiana means another excuse for sweet, sweet indulgence. The desserts of the region give ample incentive to save a little room, although in practice, this rarely happens.

Beignets

Not so much a dessert as a round-the-clock breakfast specialty akin to the common doughnut. Flat squares of dough are flash-fried to a golden, puffy glory, dusted liberally with powdered (confectioner's) sugar, and served scorching hot. Good any time of day (even after a big meal) with a cup of rich **café au lait** (see Coffee in the Drinks chapter). Ground zero for this treat is Café du Monde in the French Quarter.

Lewis displaying beignets and iced coffee, New Orleans

Bananas Foster

This now infamous dish of sliced bananas, brown sugar, spices, butter and various liqueurs was made famous at Brennan's Restaurant in the French Quarter, and is now a New Orleans sweet course standard. The sweet fruit is sauteed (usually tableside) in a flood of butter and sugar, reduced to a thick sauce, and then flamed with strong rum and a well-placed match. After the now-hackneyed show (and the flame) dies down a bit, the delicacy is served over rich vanilla ice cream. If it's your first time in New Orleans, order this at least once.

Rice pudding

Another creamy adaptation of the frugal dessert, this creamy custard has a creamy rice as its base instead of stale bread. It is usually studded with raisins and commonly found in neighborhood eateries.

Pies

The Deep South's standard dessert is usually available in several flavors and served with a cup of hot coffee. The process is simple and almost infinitely variable – a crust can be filled with fresh berries, gooey pecans, coconut cream, apples, custard, or lemon curd topped with mile-high meringue.

Coconut cream pie at The Delmonico, New Orleans

Pralines and sweet potato pie, Praline Connection, New Orleans

Bread Pudding

A specialty in New Orleans and Acadiana, this custardy creation is a good way of coaxing the family to eat leftover bread. Variations in New Orleans usually involve copious amounts of butter, eggs and cream and will usually come topped with a bourbon-spiked sugar sauce. In recent years, cooks have taken to adding white chocolate and other ingredients to spice up this simple fare, but the original, properly done, is still the best.

Fried Pies

Similar to the Central American *empanada*, fried pies are a popular convenience dessert. Flaky crust is wrapped around fruit or custard fillings, then plunged into boiling fat until the pie is crispy and hot. The best fried pies are made with a lard crust (for maximum flakiness), and are also fried in lard.

drinks
of new orleans

New Orleans maintains an international reputation for its relaxed demeanor and a perpetual willingness to celebrate. As the city rolls from party to party, it always seems to have a celebratory cocktail in its metaphorical hand.

DRINKIN' OUTTA PLASTIC: THE GO CUP

Another one of the infamous traditions of New Orleans is that of the **go cup** – an all-purpose term used for unbreakable cups that are safe for walk-and-swig consumption. It's a quirky practice for out-of-towners (who can't imagine walking about with a cocktail) and a way of life for locals (who can't imagine NOT walking with their favorite drink).

This shatterproof tradition is most obvious in Bourbon Street's pedestrian party zone. Wandering imbibers tend to drop glassware between bars, so the go cup is a decent compromise between personal freedom and inebriated safety. Although this practice is most understandable around the heavily-touristed districts, high-traffic bars around town will reflexively pour a beer or highball into a plastic cup on the assumption that you might step outside with an 'illegal' (breakable) container.

If you feel strongly about drinking out of glassware, ask the barkeep politely for a change of cup (you might even get it). If you're sipping from standard barware and feel the need to stretch your legs a bit, ask the bartender for a go cup, or risk being abruptly stopped by the bouncer on your way out.

French Quarter, New Orleans

From the quiet neighborhood beer joints to the full-blown communal revelry of the carnival season, the city has an active – and, in our experience, often gloriously excessive – drinking culture. The neon-lit bars of the French Quarter provide nonstop music and libations for the willing traveler, while farther out in the more workaday sections of town, established 'locals' provide more low-key libations and pub-style camaraderie for the natives.

Whether your pleasure is a foot-tall Mardi Gras rum drink served in an unbreakable go cup (see the boxed text Drinkin' Outta Plastic: The Go Cup) or a frosty beer to chase the peppery bite of boiled Cajun-country crawfish, there's always an ample supply (and variety) of beverages available to slake your thirst.

And since even the most dedicated revelers need a break from the harder stuff, the non-inebriating aspects of Louisiana's drinking culture are also strong, and the locals are constantly sipping strong coffee, gulping iced tea, or cooling down with root beer. With a humid climate that inspires nonstop summertime sweat, you'll revel in the wide range of beverages that soothe the parched throats of the Crescent City.

Alcoholic Drinks

In a very real sense, the decadence of New Orleans can be traced to its free flow of whiskey, beer and other high-octane treats. In the same way gourmands attempt to eat their way across the city, hard-drinking pilgrims often try to sample the countless (and often near-flammable) specialty drinks of touristy Bourbon Street.

Being historically Catholic – a religion not averse to a good stiff drink and a dance now and then – New Orleans (and the rest of French Louisiana, for that matter) is free of the anti-alcohol strictures apparent in the largely Protestant Deep South. With the exception of the deep, dark Prohibition years (1919-33), temperance was neither stylish nor sanctioned in the city. (When tee-totalling Baptists fall off their righteous water wagons, they often land in New Orleans.)

Despite its reputation for all-out bacchanal, New Orleans saves the extremes for special occasions (even in the most relaxed town, people generally have to work in the morning). Most often it's content with a few drinks at the neighborhood watering holes.

In a town where barrooms never seem to close, and even breakfast has a cocktail course, you can expect bottle-based indulgences to be plentiful and varied. Whether you prefer your poison on the rocks, on draft, in a snifter, or in a Go Cup, there will always be a range of 'adult beverages' within easy reach.

Cocktails

Wherever you have a million bartenders and a rich drinking tradition, you'll usually have a few stories that start out as follows: "You know, the cocktail was actually invented not far from here ..."

Barkeeps in New York have their version, and New Orleans locals are no different – historical conjecture just seems to go with wetting one's whistle. The local story of the cocktail's origin is a good mix of history with a pronounced French twist.

> In 1793 a young Creole apothecary named Antoine Peychaud fled the slave uprising in Santa Domingo and made his home in New Orleans. Peychaud brought with him a special recipe for aromatic bitters. He made a fortune selling his Peychaud's bitters, which he conveniently served with a measure of brandy, as a tonic for the 'stomachs sake'. Men would come into his store and take this 'tonic', which Peychaud poured into an egg cup. The French word for egg cup is *coquetier* and Peychaud's habit of serving his drink mixture from a *coquetier* is considered – at least by the locals – to be the origin of both the word cocktail and the modern jigger (the 1 ounce measure for measuring spirits).

The part about the Peychaud's bitters is well-documented – the bright red bitters are a required component of any classic Sazerac. The rest can be chalked up as either plausible history or local legend. We choose to believe the tale – providing, of course, that our elbows are resting comfortably on a cool, marble-topped French Quarter bar.

Notably absent from the following list is the **Mint Julep**, a cocktail that's more often sipped in the tippling sections of Northern Louisiana than on the stately porches of St Charles Avenue. Though this mixture of

Mint Julep on the Mississippi

bourbon, sugar, and muddled mint is often used to celebrate Derby Day (the running of the popular Kentucky horserace), it doesn't naturally occur in the bars of New Orleans, where the Sazerac (see Classic New Orleans Cocktails later in this chapter) is an appropriate substitute.

The Old Absinthe Bar on Bourbon Street, New Orleans

DRINKS

Eye Openers

Cocktails in the morning hours are a bit of decadence associated with the traditional hangover cure of 'hair of the dog that bit you,' but a New Orleans brunch (and most breakfasts in our case) wouldn't be popular without one of these selections or a more standard mimosa (champagne and orange juice).

Absinthe Suissesse A licorice-flavored legacy from the absinthe years, the Suissesse is a rich cocktail that's got more cream than kick. The subtle mix of Herbsaint (see the boxed text), heavy cream, and orgeat (primarily almond) syrup makes for a smooth start to any New Orleans morning after.

Milk Punch This innocuous-sounding concoction is a traditional holiday drink enjoyed throughout Louisiana. Like the Suissesse, milk punch has a heavy dairy base, however the addition of brandy, sugar and a little nutmeg make for a high-octane and well-spiced libation. (Bourbon may be subsituted for brandy.)

Ramos Gin Fizz Named for 19th-century New Orleans bartender Henry Ramos, this rich, frothy cocktail is a popular brunch beverage. The astringent flavor of gin is fortified with a foamy mixture of cream, egg white, extra-fine sugar, fizzy water and, the distinctive ingredient, a subtle splash of orange-flower water.

Bloody Mary A well-known combination of tomato juice spiked with vodka and peppery flavorings. As you might expect in the land of pepper sauce, 'bloodies' here are a bit on the fiery side and the traditional celery garnish is often replaced with peppery pickled green beans and carrots. The vodka isn't the only ingredient that will wake you up here.

HERBSAINT

When absinthe, the insanely popular licorice-flavored liqueur, was outlawed in the early 20th century for its extreme addictive and psychoactive potential, cultures worldwide tried to find a substitute for the bitter liquor. The French developed *pastis* and Pernod as safer alternatives to the wormwood-based absinthe. Not to be outdone, a New Orleans company developed its own wormwood-free absinthe with star anise replacing the forbidden herb.

The resulting yellowish-green Herbsaint replaced absinthe in cocktails and culinary preparations alike. A host of local specialties use Herbsaint as a primary ingredient or subtle flavoring, including local versions of Oysters Rockefeller and the New Orleans signature cocktails such as the Sazerac and Absinthe Suissesse.

Classic New Orleans Cocktails

Often served at the older bars and restaurants around town, these classic cocktails represent the best of old-school New Orleans cocktail culture. Though each of these drinks have internationally known counterparts (Old Fashioned, gin and tonic, and Irish coffee, respectively), these concoctions require a slightly adventurous palate and a sense of local history. New Orleans' bars wouldn't be the same without either.

The Sazerac Another 'old New Orleans' trademark drink, the Sazerac is a potent whiskey drink that uses either rye or bourbon as its primary ingredient. Recipes differ, but the originals use two kinds of aromatic bitters (including the locally-produced Peychaud's), a bit of sugar, and a swish of Herbsaint for telltale licorice flavoring. This classic cocktail is served on the rocks or straight up and is garnished with a lemon twist. Best prepared by a bartender who is at least 70 years old.

Pimm's Cup A warm-season refresher most often associated with the infamous French Quarter bar, Napoleon House. Pimm's Cup is a simple mix of the British gin-based liqueur (Pimm's No 1) topped with soda or ginger ale . The traditional garnishes on this wonderfully cooling highball drink are lemon wedges and cucumber slices. In a pinch Pimm's Cup can be considered a liquid salad course.

Cafe Brulot More of an after-dinner experience than a cocktail, Cafe Brulot – or its longer name Cafe Brulot Diabolique – is another New Orleans tableside 'light and serve' preparation (see also Bananas Foster under Desserts in the Staples & Specialties chapter). Spices, sugar, and brandy are heated to the flaming point and ignited for dramatic effect; strong brewed coffee is then added.

Pimm's Cup at Napoleon House, New Orleans

DRINKS

Tourist Drinks

Poured freely from the storefront bars of Bourbon Street, these drinks are standards for those hell bent on a French Quarter party experience. Much-imitated, and often more festive than substantial, these libations have contributed to many tales of blurry Mardi Gras mayhem.

The Hurricane Made famous by the French Quarter bar – and tourist institution – Pat O'Brien's, this towering rum drink can be spotted from a mile away. Bright pink from its primary ingredient (passion fruit juice), the Hurricane is served in a foot-tall glass in the shape of a curvy storm lamp.

The Frozen Daiquiri In other cities, bartenders would recognize this name as Hemingway's trademark lime and rum cocktail, but here the word 'daiquiri' takes on a much wider, and looser, definition.

Frozen daiquiris are a class of hyper-cooled beverages that are somewhere between a drink and shaved ice, liberally mixed with just about any liquor. Walk-by bars on Bourbon Street and other infamous party zones house banks of whirling machines in all the colors of the rainbow. These magic machines pump out quiescently frozen daiquiris, icy White Russians (vodka, Kahlua and cream concoctions), and bright green Margaritas and a host of other potent drinks laced with high-proof rum or Everclear (pure grain alcohol). Owing to bulk consumption and walk-away clientele, these 'bars' tend to use powdered mixes and cheap, hangover-inducing liquors. And even if you *know* they're of questionable quality, a tall plastic cup of frozen daiquiri is still nigh impossible to resist on a stifling hot day.

NEW ORLEANS RUM

Rum – a liquor distilled from fermented sugar juice – originally came from early trade with the West Indies, and it seems only natural that Louisiana should develop a rum from the fruits of its prosperous sugar country. Besides, many of New Orleans' trademark tourist drinks (especially the Hurricane) are based on the stuff so why not make it here instead of importing from Puerto Rico, Jamaica, or Barbados?

In 1995, local entrepreneurs with a taste for the Caribbean started producing New Orleans Rum (also known by its initials NO).

Not your average rotgut grog, NO Rum uses Louisiana sugarcane (a more expensive, though accessible ingredient) in its mash, and takes a few cues from distillers of latter day 'super premium' whiskies. The distilled rum is aged in oak barrels for three years, which makes it more of a full-flavored sipping spirit than a mixing liquor. But taken in a snifter or in a cocktail, it's another local product that's well worth sampling. Repeatedly, if time allows …

Bourbon Street, French Quarter, New Orleans

COCKTAIL RECIPES
Cafe Brulot

If you try preparing this cocktail at home, be especially careful when mixing intoxicants and open flame. Keep a fire extinguisher handy, just for safety's sake.

Ingredients

4	cloves
1	short cinnamon stick
3 lumps	sugar
2 jiggers	brandy
2 cups	strong hot coffee
	lemon peel

Incorporate all the ingredients except the coffee in a flameproof bowl. Dim the lights, ignite the brandy and let the mixture burn for a minute or so, stirring gently. Slowly add the coffee, stirring all the while, until the flame dies. Serve (and wonder why, when you make it yourself, it's never quite as good as it was at the restaurant).
Serves 2

DRINKS

Cocktails at Commander's Palace, New Orleans:
Mint Julep, Sazerac, Hurricane, Milk Punch and Bloody Mary

Sazerac

Ingredients

2 fl oz (60ml)	rye whiskey
1 tsp	sugar syrup
3 dashes	Peychauds bitters
3 dashes	Angostura bitters
3 dashes	Herbsaint (or an anisette such as Ricard or Pernod)
lemon twist	

Incorporate all the ingredients except the Herbsaint and lemon twist in a shaker with ice. Pour the Pernod into a chilled old-fashioned glass and coat the inside of the glass. Pour off any excess. Rub the lemon twist on the rim, strain the whiskey mixture into the glass and garnish with the twist.
    Serves 1

Hurricane

Ingredients

1 fl oz (30ml)	lemon juice
4 fl oz (135ml)	dark rum
2 fl oz (60ml)	fruit cocktail or other fruit juice (passionfruit and orange juice is the preferred mix and it should be sweetened).
1	orange slice
1	maraschino cherry

Fill a hurricane glass with ice and pour over the ingredients. Garnish with a slice of orange and a maraschino cherry. If you do not have a hurricane glass use any tall glass or a brandy balloon.
    Serves 1

Spicy Bloody Mary Mix

Ingredients

1 quart (1 liter)	tomato juice
2 tblsp	Worcestershire sauce
1 tsp	prepared horseradish (or to taste)
1 tblsp	Louisiana pepper sauce (or to taste)
1 tsp	celery salt
	sprinkle of garlic powder
	juice of one lime
1 fl oz (30ml)	vodka per drink

Mix all non-alcoholic ingredients and refrigerate. When ready to serve, pour over ice and add 1 fl oz (30ml) of vodka per drink. Garnish with pickled okra or marinated green beans. Makes 4-5 cocktails.

Bloody Mary mix provided by Stephan Este

DRINKS

Beer

Gallon for gallon, beer is Louisiana's most popular alcoholic drink and as such, the mandatory beverage at impromptu crawfish boils. Throughout the state, local street carnivals and street festivals float on a floodtide of inexpensive, fizzy lager. Plastic cups slosh with standard American pilsner – the low-alcohol, mild brew that qualifies as the American industrial standard, along with its extra-watery 'lite' counterpart. The usual mega-breweries (Budweiser, Miller, Coors) have largely replaced local producers, including the venerable Jax Brewery, which is now an upscale French Quarter shopping mall. Not that Jax's beer was that great, but at least it was indigenous.

New Orleans' most famous surviving brewery is Dixie, founded in 1907. The flavor of the flagship beer isn't noticeably different from the national brands but it's worth reaching for a cold Dixie 'long neck' for a local change. Dixie also produces a couple of other mystique-heavy beers – Blackened Voodoo lager and Jazz Amber Lite – which are longer on image than taste.

Thanks to the nationwide microbrew boom in the 1980s, New Orleans has some worthy locally-produced beers to call its own. The most widespread brands hail from the Abita Brewery (see the boxed text) and are now on draft across Louisiana. Other good bets include local brewpubs such as the Crescent City Brewhouse in the French Quarter.

ABITA SPRINGS ETERNAL

The former spa town of Abita Springs lies 30 miles north of New Orleans across the lake-skimming Pontchartrain Bridge. The natural springs that attracted health-conscious vacationers to the area are still burbling, but now provide water for the more vital commodity of Abita Beer.

This microbrewery produced its first batch in 1986 and has been pumping out fresh, flavorful beers ever since. From its standard amber ale to more ambitious Mardi Gras bock and seasonal Jockimo stout, Abita beers provide a welcome local alternative to the usual corporate lagers.

The boys at Abita are also canny enough to play the intriguing name game with their products; try the dark and malty TurboDog, or the raspberry-enhanced wheat beer Purple Haze for size. Abita's brewers also vary their offerings according to season by offering a nice bock beer during Mardi Gras, an autumnal Oktoberfest brew, and a thick stout to chase off the winter chill.

The brewery also bottles a micro-brewed root beer sweetened with cane sugar rather than the more prevalent corn sweeteners.

The once-tiny concern now boasts an adjoining pub and restaurant. Brewery tours (complete with ample samples) are available on weekends.

DRINKS

Local beer, Blackened Voodoo Lager

Wine

Broadly speaking, the wine culture of Louisiana is more evident in fine dining establishments than in everyday culinary contexts. The bold flavors of Cajun-influenced dishes are distinctly beer-friendly, and the lack of local vineyards make wine drinking much more the exception than the rule. Neighborhood Creole-Italian joints will usually have a standard house red served by the glass – usually an inexpensive jug chianti or merlot – as a nod to their Mediterranean motherland.

As you'd expect from any city known for its fine dining, New Orleans' high-end restaurants come well equipped with world-class wine cellars. Many of the fancier establishments maintain stocks of worldwide vintages that number in the thousands.

Generally, the wines savored in New Orleans' fine restaurants have been shipped in from far afield as the humid conditions of the region are unsuitable for the growing of wine grapes. Wine lists will instead be dominated by products of the world's established wine-growing regions (especially those of France and the emerging California vineyards).

Traditionally, simple wines were made from local fruits such as strawberries, dewberries and muscadine grapes. This relatively sweet wine is generally associated with country folks looking to make the best out of a naturally occurring resource. In the river port border town of Nachez, Mississippi vintners produce a commercial version of this largely home-grown specialty drink. Look for it particularly in the northern parts of the state.

Muscadine grapes, Mississippi

Cherry Bounce

A popular homemade cordial common throughout the state is cherry bounce, made by slow-steeping very ripe cherries in a sugar and alcohol mixture – vodka or brandy being the usual choices – for at least a month. While steeping, the mixture is kept in a cool, dark place. When sufficiently brewed, the mixture is strained through cheesecloth and poured into decorative decanters or empty whiskey bottles. Usually served in petite liqueur glasses, cherry bounce is a special occasion cocktail, often used to commemorate major family events.

The practice is akin to the historical Creole tradition of making **ratafia**, a similar fruit-based cordial used as digestifs either after dinner or between courses in extended Creole celebratory meals.

Non-Alcoholic Drinks
Coffee

Dark, strong and free-flowing, Louisiana's characteristic coffee is a soothing yet powerful way to start the day. Visitors to Louisiana often comment on the strength of the mud-like coffee served in homes and restaurants throughout the region, and many city and country traditions are based on this simple hot beverage.

In greater New Orleans, you're likely to find chicory coffee served as the milky **café au lait**, the specialty brew of the French Quarter's illustrious Café du Monde. On your first morning in the French Quarter kick-start the day with a visit to the Decatur Street institution. Here you'll find perhaps the best coffee in town – deep, dark, smoky French-roasted chicory coffee, cut with equal parts of hot milk – and the gold standard of local beignets. Conveniently, this 'original coffee stand' is open round the clock, so you can feed the urge whenever it strikes.

Chicory, a roasted herb root, is often mixed with ground coffee, resulting in **Creole coffee** or **New Orleans blend**. Originally used to 'extend' scarce coffee beans (some say by Napoleon's armies), chicory is added for a fuller-bodied coffee and has a pungent flavor reminiscent of marijuana smoke. This flavor can be an acquired taste for even the most dedicated dark-roast drinker. Only a few brave souls (usually locals) brave the extra kick of chicory sans milk, favoring the richer texture provided by the root.

Farther afield in the state's Cajun region, your cup of coffee won't have that distinctive chicory 'whang' but it will be plenty strong. Cajun coffee, usually dark roasted and slow-dripped, is sometimes said to be "thick enough to stand a spoon in." Milk (if any is added) will usually be heated in a small stovetop pot.

European settlers first brought coffee and New Orleans has been one of the world's largest importers ever since. The Creoles believed coffee had digestive, medicinal and pronounced economic qualities; many Creole fortunes were made trading in the popular beans.

The most popular commercial coffee brands are Café du Monde (or CDM in local slang) for chicory lovers, and Community Coffee for fans of standard dark roast.

Iced tea

In hot and humid Louisiana, iced tea is more than just a drink – it's a miracle weapon against blistering seasonal heat and afternoon workday doldrums. The cooling caffeinated beverage accounts for 80 percent of tea consumed in the United States and is a standard offering during summer meals. If it weren't for bucket-sized tumblers of the crisp, invigorating treat, we think the economies of the Hot Zone might grind to an overheated halt.

DRINKS

Preparation of the common beverage couldn't be simpler – it's simply cold regular tea served in long glasses topped off with ice. Garnished either with citrus slices or flavorful mint leaves – no milk, please – a towering, sweaty tumbler of tea is commonly served with afternoon and evening meals.

In Northern Louisiana, you may be asked to specify whether you want 'sweet tea' – iced tea that's been super-charged with pounds of pure sugar. This peculiarly Deep Southern variation on the theme isn't suggested for diabetics or anyone who doesn't have a mouth full of sweet teeth.

When you order iced tea at a restaurant, it is usually a bottomless cup and will be regularly refilled. If you want a proper English cup of tea, specify 'hot tea' or you'll get a tall, ice-filled glass instead of a steaming mug.

Root Beer

The Native Americans made tea from the roots of the sassafras tree and it is from this original usage that root beer owes its creation. These days, Louisianans drink twice as much root beer as the American average. This is largely due to the local Barq's root beer, created by Ed Barq in 1898 at his home in nearby Biloxi, Mississippi. This carbonated New Orleans institution goes well with the hot weather and full-flavored food. Barq's is widely available in cans and bottles, and is the only local brand although it was recently acquired by The Coca-Cola company. Although sold as a soft drink, it's not nearly as sweet as regular sodas.

Traditionally, root beer in a Cajun home or country restaurant would be mixed from a concentrated syrup (usually Zatarain's) rather than coming from a post-mix machine or carbonated bottle. However, this practice is fading because of cheap modern bottling and distribution.

W.H. Tupper General Merchandise Museum, Jennings, Louisiana

Water & Mineral Water

Water will be automatically brought to the table at most eateries, and it will be either tap or filtered but always well chilled. It's technically safe to drink although the taste has little to recommend it (see the Fit & Healthy chapter).

Bottled water is readily available although there doesn't seem to be much of a demand for the sparkling variety.

Kaldi's Coffee House on Decatur Street, French Quarter, New Orleans

Soft Drinks

You'll find the usual range of globally recognized carbonated soft drinks here, but New Orleans also has its own home-grown fizzy beverages – the diverse (and strangely flavored) Big Shot brand. If you peruse the drink coolers in local convenience stores, you may find such offbeat treasures as Big Shot Grape, Honey Dew Mist, or Ohana Orange Punch.

Fountain drinks are available just about everywhere and are currently undergoing severe portion inflation. Be warned: don't ask for a 'large' soft drink unless you want enough to fill a bucket.

DRINKS

home cooking
& traditions

While New Orleans has one of the most distinct restaurant scenes in the US, its home kitchens often conform to the American standard. It's in rural Cajun Country, however, where you'll find Louisiana's most active and vibrant home cooking culture – hospitality and culinary dash are essential hallmarks of Southern Louisiana homes.

Since the end of World War II, the modern American kitchen has been a place of social and culinary transition. Twentieth century conveniences replaced the wood-burning stoves of yore and more women entered the full-time work force. Faceless supermarkets replaced local food specialists and the television supplanted the kitchen table as the household's social focal point. With the passing of time, American food culture has become more homogenous and the importance of kitchen traditions has decreased.

In Louisiana, however, home cooking traditions are still alive and well. In New Orleans, the city's rich, multi-layered restaurant selection detracts somewhat from home cooking traditions, as many family occasions are celebrated in favorite restaurants instead of at the communal table. But farther out in the country – especially in Cajun Acadiana – fewer restaurants means more action in the everyday kitchen. Friends gather around the stove before informal dinners, stirring and smelling the pots before sitting down to eat. Casual afternoon visits spur friendly conversation and impromptu midafternoon snacks around the kitchen table. And of course, a family's coffee pot rarely sits idle – if a friend approaches, cups fill and stories spin.

In pre-modern days, the household kitchen was built around a simple wood-burning iron stove – essentially a campfire in a cast-iron box – which provided extreme heat without insulation or temperature control. When the stove was stoked and burning, the house and cook were likely over-heated, especially during Louisiana's tropical summertimes. Kitchen fires caused by the stoves' unchecked heat were also common occurrences. To minimize overheating and devastating building fires, kitchens often stood apart from the 'main house' in separate buildings.

During the state's colonial times, wealthy families living in the town-houses of New Orleans or upriver antebellum plantations had the luxury of help in the kitchen. At first, female African slaves prepared family meals. Once slavery was consigned to history, many of these women continued in their domestic roles, albeit now as paid workers. In the city, these pioneering cooks prepared the everyday family meals and the elaborate seven-course Creole banquets that were then in fashion. Even today, economically advantaged families sometimes have hired kitchen workers.

Without strong traditions of kitchen help or urban restaurant scenes, Cajun Southern Louisiana maintains consistently strong ties to both the home kitchen and family table. Large family events are much more likely to be celebrated with a meal at the house than with a visit to a restaurant. The kitchen table (rather than the TV room) is the social center of a household – a place where parents drink their morning coffee, children take their daily meals, and whole families gather to socialize and eat (see the boxed text Crowded Tables & Blood Tomatoes later in this chapter). In Cajun

The old stove in the kitchen of Olga Manuel, Eunice

Country, visitors usually enter the house through the kitchen door to the side or back of the house, while other more formal spaces (fancy dining areas and living rooms) go largely unused.

In most cases, it's Mama who does most of the food shopping and planning, but food – especially its preparation and consumption – is very much a family affair. The children of the house grow up helping in the kitchen and kitchen skills – from making a simple roux to boiling large quantities of crawfish at a family crawfish boil – are cultural lessons that children learn from watching their parents and grandparents. A fisherman's young daughter knows that at the end of her father's trawling run, she will be sorting shrimp by size and peeling the fresh shellfish for freezing. The son of an avid gardener knows how to prepare string beans for the pot and slice okra for gumbo. And all children are taught, at a tender age, how to gather pecans as they litter the ground in fall and winter. Older kids and their parents then spend hours cracking and shelling the tasty nuts for snacking and cooking.

Louisiana men are also very proud of their cooking skills, many of which are modern-day adaptations of rustic wilderness/campfire cookery. In many cases, post-hunt game preparation is recreated at outdoor celebrations using quasi-industrial cooking tools (see Special Utensils later in this chapter). While the Mama generally reigns over the indoor kitchen, the men rule their improvised outdoor kitchens. Cajun men are in their element when cooking large-scale specialties, and at a big family gathering, there's plenty of culinary bragging and friendly rivalry as the males gather round the fire.

Rosedown Plantation, St Francisville

HOME COOKING

With the advent of the supermarket, Louisiana's raw materials are more likely to be pre-packaged than home-grown (see the Shopping & Markets chapter). The Cajun home pantry is likely to be filled with mostly store bought products, with an emphasis on locally-produced goods such as Community coffee, seasoning blend from the local meat market, Zatarain's Creole mustard, and Steen's cane syrup. Among the usual staples (flour, sugar, breakfast cereals and canned goods) will be the homemade treasures – jars full of 'canned' edibles from friends or family. Plentiful fruit and vegetables are picked at the peak of the season and can be 'put up' in the form of peach jelly, dewberry jam, pickled okra or fig preserves.

You Know You're From New Orleans When......

* Your idea of a cruise ship is the Canal Street Ferry, and a foreign cruise ship is the Chalmette Ferry.
* You can cross 2 lanes of traffic and U-turn through a neutral ground while avoiding 2 joggers and a streetcar, then fit into the oncoming traffic flow while never touching the brakes.
* You wonder what Anne Rice has against a building that looks like a Mardi Gras float.
* You think "drinking water" when you look at the Mississippi River.
* You know where you got your shoes.
* You're out of town and ask where the drive-thru daiquiri place is and they look at you like you have three heads.
* You consider having a good meal as your birthright.
* You like your crawfish so hot, you can't distinguish between sweat, snot and crawfish juice.

A bit of local humour found at the Dry Dock Bar & Cafe, Algiers

Since many of these products are available at supermarkets, the practice continues as a labor of love and gift-giving tradition across the state. Gifts of food – tomatoes from friends with gardens, friends who fish, friends who hunt – are commonplace and important sources of fresh materials and communal hospitality.

In terms of cookbooks, the average Louisiana kitchen usually contains a couple of basic texts, but rarely anything beyond the American standards – a copy of the local Junior League cookbook (popular titles include *Talk about Good* and *River Road Recipes*), possibly an old, dog-eared edition of *The Joy of Cooking* – and a file folder containing handwritten recipe cards, and yellowing newspaper clippings. In general, Louisiana cooks rely on simple dishes and kitchen intuition for their everyday cooking. Many standards of the Louisiana repertoire – from red beans and rice to smothered pork chops to okra and tomatoes – are basic enough to be transmitted without complex written instructions.

HOME COOKING

Special Utensils

By and large, the utensils of the Louisiana kitchen don't differ much from those of any modern American home. In any Louisiana cupboard, you're likely to find a standard set of pots, skillets, cookie sheets and roasting pans – with a few notable exceptions.

Shelves and shelves of Louisiana hot sauce

In most parts of the state, you'll see cookware made of 'black iron', heavy cast iron that's known for its heat retention, natural non-stick properties and sometimes awkward weight. Since the 1950s, lighter aluminum cookware has become plentiful and cheap, effectively replacing cast iron. Before the Aluminum Age, it wasn't uncommon for home cooks to use a row of specialized cast-iron vessels from slope-sided Dutch ovens (deep pots) to deep chicken-frying skillets. But today you're still likely to find at least one cast-iron implement, often a family heirloom, in a Louisiana kitchen.

Tools of the trade, New Orleans

HOME COOKING

BISCUIT TORTURE

Somewhere through a perfectly good dream state, a gravelly voice rasps out "Aaa-reee-ZAY! Aaa-reee-ZAY!" and seconds later I feel the bedside lamp burning sharp holes in my eyelids.

These two not-so-pleasurable sensations came as no surprise to me – after all, I was in my grandfather's house – but the primal pain of a pre-dawn wakeup is always a shock. That is, of course, unless you're Achilles Leon Hebert (Papá to his grandkids) who, at age 80, still got a sadistic charge out of waking his family from deep slumber.

"You want to make biscuits?" Short pause. "Then GET UP." Shorter pause. "Aaaa-reee-ZAY!!" That last word, which loosely translates to 'arise' in Cajun French, was the bane of our family's late risers.

"Mmmmm … rrrrr." I gave my traditional reply to his high-volume bellow and followed him into the kitchen. We both shuffled across hardwood floors in the pre-dawn darkness. The previous night, I asked him to wake me up early and teach me how to make his famous biscuits. The important lessons, it seems, are not without painful consequences.

Papá's biscuits are the stuff of family legend. They emerge from the oven perfectly round, light for their size and melt-in-your-mouth tender. When grandchildren came to visit, he'd make a double batch for breakfast, served with plenty of sweet butter and floating in dark Steen's cane syrup along with pounds of crispy fried bacon. Even the perpetually sleepy could make it out of bed for Papá's biscuits. In the summer months, when the Ponchatoula strawberries were in the local markets, Papá would add a little more sugar, cut the disks bigger, and make the perfect base for sweet strawberry shortcake.

As the son of Cajun Catholics who 'emigrated' to the Northern Louisiana city of Shreveport, Leon learned how to make this traditional bread of the Deep South as a young man and prepared it on special occasions. As a crossover food for his family and his childrens' families, his mother's recipe bridged the gap between Louisiana's Anglo and French cultures and the generational cultures within his own family.

Papá shuffled his way around the kitchen making coffee and preparing for the task ahead. The kettle whistled, he filled up his aging French drip coffee pot, and soon we were sipping thick, strong coffee. One cup with a little heated milk to 'take the edge off', and we were ready.

"Start off with a bunch of flour," he mumbled while scooping an unmeasured cup into the huge jar. "And put it in the sifter." He took out a battered set of aluminum measuring spoons. "Add the baking soda and baking powder. Then a little bit of sugar, and some salt. And sift."

"Wait a minute," I had to stop him. I looked at my notepad, which had a column of ingredients, but no measurements. No numbers whatsoever.

"How much do you mean?"

"How much what?" he replied.

"Ummm … Flour?" Starting at the top seemed to make the most sense.

"This much" he said, lifting the bowl so I could see.

"One cup? Two cups?" At this time of the morning – still nowhere near first light– my eye/brain coordination was shot to hell.

"Awww, hell. I don't know." He wrinkled his bald-headed brow and motioned to the dented flour scoop. "Two of those."

It had obviously been years since he'd explained the process to anyone. Papá added the ingredients intuitively – in his mind, the ingredients just went together the same way they always did.

The motion of cutting in the shortening, the mixing of the buttermilk, the rolling and cutting of the biscuit dough – none of these were ever written down, and a written recipe never really entered his mind. I watched him go through the whole process without writing a thing. After he had placed the first batch of biscuits in the oven and the kitchen had filled up with the aroma of fresh baking, we started another batch – this time pausing as I translated his intuition into cups, teaspoons, and ounces. I found out how much salt Papá could fit between his fingers and how long a splash made for the right amount of buttermilk. And then, as I rolled and cut my own circular biscuits, I started to understand his vague directions. After my first hot biscuits came out of the oven I answered my own questions.

How much do you add? Just enough.

How long do you cook it? Long enough.

When are they finished? When they're done.

Not very specific, but good enough to make good biscuits. At the end, I had a rough recipe and a plate full of freshly buttered biscuits. Crunching in to the bready browned disks, I was relieved to finally know the secret of the biscuit. Papá went to get ready for work and after another cup of thick muddy coffee, I had time for a nap before sunrise.

Pableaux Johnson

Leon's 5am Biscuits

First, get out of bed and wander to the kitchen at an ungodly hour in the morning. Since the grand tradition of biscuit-baking is passed from the elders of the clan (who wake up early anyway) to the younger members (who would just as soon sleep till noon), the early wake-up is essential to the pure physical torture that always proceeds the most profound of spiritual pilgrimages. And it's worth it.

Preheat the oven to 450ºF (250ºC). Sift together 2 cups of flour, 2 heaped tablespoons of baking powder, a pinch of salt, and a little bit of sugar. Cut 2 heaped tablespoons of Crisco into the dry mix with pastry thang or back of spoon until tacky. Then add 1-1½ cups of buttermilk and mix until doughy. Roll out gently on floured wax paper or cloth. Cut out with glass or biscuit cutter. Put on oiled pan. Bake until done. Deal with the vagueness.

Proper cornbread, so crucial to the Soul Food and Southern country-style traditions of Northern Louisiana, can only be made in a cast-iron skillet. If you have ever crunched into a perfectly browned crust of homemade buttermilk cornbread, then you surely know the difference that cast iron makes in the creation of this staple. Likewise, it's nearly impossible to make a proper roux without a heavy bottomed Dutch oven that holds the heat during the long, slow browning process. As a result, most of the standards of a Cajun kitchen start off in the revered 'roux pot'. Despite falling from fashion, cast-iron cookware is still produced and can be easily purchased at any local hardware store. This cookware requires only minimal maintenance – thorough drying and the occasional rubdown with vegetable oil – and beats the fancier (as well as more expensive) pans for both heat retention and value.

Cooking rabbit stew, Eunice

Many families in Louisiana keep a 'crawfish rig' in the garage for large-scale cooking events. This imposing apparatus consists of a freestanding burner on a welded-iron tripod set at roughly waist height. This burner is powered by a tank of compressed propane gas and ranks as the most important outdoor cooking tool in Cajun culture. At full flame, these burners produce a loud roar and incredible amounts of heat. These rigs are capable of heating up 15-gallon crawfish pots or vats of 'fish frying oil' in a matter of minutes. As the perfect marriage of industrial technology and culinary experimentation, crawfish rigs are the oilfield's gift to the Cajun cook.

SUNDAY AFTERNOON CRAB BOIL

Jacques' family invited me to their Sunday seafood boil on the proviso that I would participate in all aspects of the event for the full cultural experience. This was some comfort as I found myself hungover, and on the road at dawn, after a particularly colorful night in New Orleans.

We headed northeast from New Orleans in the glowing green light that only live oak limbs hirsute with Spanish moss and roadside bayous can create. My senses slowly awakened as I sipped a café au lait and nibbled on a beignet. Three of us sat in silence as the bayou snaked along beside us. Ninety minutes of broken white lines later, we are in Yscloskey, a small fishing town on Bayou la Loutre. The boats had just returned and the fishermen were unloading their catch. Jacques' father, Andre, is greeted by name; he's a valued customer who has been buying his fish here since he was a young man.

It was summer and we were buying live crabs. Andre negotiated to buy 30 of them, and got some ice to keep them fresh. Further down the road, we picked up a dozen soft-shell crabs. The activity had aroused us, and Jacques and his father talked excitedly about crabbing and former seafood expeditions. We took a detour to another seafood supplier, whose seafood boil has been a family favorite ever since there was a family. The recipe is a secret; customers have given up trying to find out the ingredients, just as long as the supply is assured. Finally, we stopped at the local supermarket to pick up some seafood seasoning (a mixture of cornstarch, wheat flour and seasonings) with which to coat the soft-shell crabs and, while we're here, corn, small potatoes and plenty of beer.

The homestead was a hive of activity. Andre took charge of the boil, firing up the gas burner and filling the large pot with water. While it came to the boil he shucked the corn and readied the ingredients he needed. Jacques' mother, Pat, prepared the soft-shell crabs in the kitchen, removing the unwanted grisly bits with scissors. The seasonal crustaceans were coated in the seasoning and placed in the fridge. With the preparations in place, we covered the table and patio with newspaper (so we just wrap up the debris) and cracked open the first beers.

With the water bubbling excitedly, the boil seasoning was added and, after a few stirs of the wooden paddle, the crabs were plopped into the cauldron. Pat raced off to prepare her scurry of soft-shell crabs.

As soon as her bounty hit the table, it disappeared among reaching hands, the last energetic spell of the afternoon. We ate the soft-shell crabs whole, which sated our appetites just enough so we could pick the boiled crabs apart at a pace befitting a Sunday afternoon.

Hours, five crabs, and countless beers later, seafood boil oozes down my arms and I sit behind a small pyramid of crab shells – relaxed, content and privileged.

Charmaine O'Brien

CROWDED TABLES & BLOOD TOMATOES

It was one of those great childhood mysteries. As far as her grandchildren were concerned, Mamá cooked the best food in the whole world. Her garlic-spiked roast beef, rice and gravy could make the angels weep. She fixed yellow squash so tender and delicious that normally finicky eaters fought to empty the pot. She could turn to the stove and create just about anything in ungodly quantity, but her favorite summertime meal was probably her simplest – a plateful of thick Creole tomato slices seasoned with a single sprinkle of salt.

Like most women of her generation, Lorelle Seal Hebert ran a high-traffic high-volume kitchen with a table that was never quite empty. As the mother of eight and grandmother of 25, she could feed the Mongol hordes at a moment's notice and still have plenty left over for dinner time. Her refrigerator contained rows of magical makeshift Tupperware capable of bringing forth impossible amounts of food, enough to just 'throw together' a midday meal for whoever stopped by within an hour of mealtime. When a caller heard her battle cry – "You going to eat with us?" – they knew the decision had already been made.

Summer lunches were an edible three-ring circus, with kids jumping around the chairs, adults passing and serving platters of pork roast and potato salad, and Mamá acting as the kitchen ringmaster. With a quick command (bordering on sweet but unmistakably direct) she could instruct a grown daughter to make an iceberg salad or send a hyperactive grandkid to fetch another jar of her homemade mayonnaise. Under her direction, the family became both a smoothly-choreographed kitchen crew and well-fed guests of honor. After all, you had to work if you wanted to eat.

While the assembled throng munched their way through endless plates of cool cucumber salads and anything over Louisiana rice, Lorelle kept moving in the background, filling the table with "just one more thing." Still working with her back turned to the table, she would tell whole stories through my mostly-deaf grandfather ("Tell 'em about the new tractor, Daddy. Tell 'em."), stopping only to wrap a moist hug around the smallest grandchild in attendance. Cries of "Come eat with us" were met with a pitcher of tea to pass or calls for "another helping."

Mamá maintained this constant, energetic hover until the last diner pushed back from the table in bloated defeat. The biggest eater at the table usually drew her attention ("Now look at that boy EAT!") and signaled the end of the meal. After a few minutes of post-mealtime coma, she'd whip the crew into reverse action – washing plates, re-stocking the fridge, and clearing the table for the next meal.

"Go on, now. I love you but you need to go." With the kitchen restored to semi-order, Lorelle subtly cleared the room for her favorite

A home in the French Quarter, New Orleans

meal and post-lunch quiet time. Stopover guests would wobble off to home or work. Far-flung cousins would head out to play (or to nap if they'd been bad). And our perpetually moving hostess would sit down to her pleasantly solitary midday meal.

Unnaturally heavy and deep red, Mamá's prized Creole tomatoes were the best in the world and her trademark summer lunch. Once nicked with the house's only 'sharp knife', the huge beefsteak monsters left pools of tart juice over every possible surface – cutting boards, stoneware serving platters, and the chins of enthusiastic eaters. She would cut the vine-ripened beauties into maybe four slices apiece – thick slabs of tangy perfection– and arrange them on her plate.

Lorelle tried to grow tomatoes like these herself – a few token plants in her flowerbeds – but invariably stocked up through the generosity of her vegetable-gardening friends. They'd come by as long as their plants were producing – always carrying a grocery bag full of their overflow. "Well, Lorelle, we just can't eat 'em all." they'd say, "and everybody know how you like your tomatoes."

She liked them big, ripe, and (most importantly) eaten in the quiet of early afternoon. Even though the grandkids were banished outside or to a restless naptime, we'd sneak back and peek into the kitchen. An hour before, Mama managed to feed 15 guests within an inch of their lives. And now, with an empty table and a single blood-red plate, she took her solitary summertime reward. One slow, quiet bite at a time, with just a pinch of salt.

Pableaux Johnson

celebrating
with food

Eating, drinking and dancing – you'll rarely encounter an event in Louisiana that doesn't include at least two of the three. In fact, food and drink are often reason enough for a celebration. Whether you've worked up an appetite cheering at a parade, dancing at a Cajun *fais do do* (street dance) or watching a small town hog slaughter, you can be assured that the festivities will include plenty of regionally unique food.

The Mardi Gras Season

If you think the world needs a shake up, that kings should dance with street kids and the rich should throw their wealth to the masses, even if you want to eat babies and steal greased pigs, then don your party regalia, or get naked, and head for Mardi Gras. This is when every facet of New Orleans' culture collides in a feast for your senses, and for your stomach.

Mardi Gras is the 'be all and end all' of New Orleans parties and a season of celebration and tradition throughout French Louisiana. Members of Mardi Gras **krewes** (exclusive social societies) organize the city's trademark parades and fling aluminum coins into the howling crowds. Waving celebrities crowned 'king for a day' throw faux jewelry from the elaborate floats that crawl along New Orleans' streets. Members of working class black communities mobilize their 'Social Aid and Pleasure Clubs' and take to the streets elaborately costumed as 'Mardi Gras Indians' accompanied by a powerful entourage of percussionists. Costumed (and appropriately drunken) revelers transform the French Quarter into a seething spectacle of glittering humanity. Female revelers use quick flashes of nudity (a momentary lift of the shirt) to inspire spontaneous showers of plastic beads and catcalls. Harlequins, body-painted drag queens and last-minute maskers push elbow-to-elbow through the Quarter's streets, which slosh in an ankle-deep 'soup' of trash, beer, discarded food, and various bodily fluids.

New Orleans' infamous Mardi Gras party has distant roots in pre-Christian Pagan times, when uninhibited debauchery marked springtime fertility celebrations. Greeks, Romans and assorted Druids all celebrated the end of winter with wild, fleshy abandon. In a can't-beat-them-join-them-move, the Catholic Church incorporated these festivals into the Christian liturgical calendar to mark the last day before Lent's culinary clamp-down. It was at this time that the Latin term *carnevale* (farewell to the flesh) was born. The Lenten season begins on the church holiday of Ash Wednesday, so the decadent day before became known as Shrove Tuesday in English, or Mardi Gras (Fat Tuesday) in French. Over time, the Carnival took on a more theatrical air with the incorporation of masked balls and elaborate community festivals, especially in heavily Catholic Latin cultures. The more uninhibited celebrations of Carnival have survived in places like Brazil's Rio De Janeiro and the streets of New Orleans. However, never content with a single-day celebration, the denizens of French Louisiana stretch their party out for the entire Carnival season – lasting from the fixed holiday of the Twelfth Night until Mardi Gras proper. (Since the Lenten cycle is linked directly to the Jewish lunar calendar, Mardi Gras is a movable feast that can fall on any date from early February to early March.)

Beads and baubles on the balcony, New Orleans

The food traditions of Mardi Gras are as varied as its costumed revelers. The sweetest tradition is the King cake, a sugared ring of glazed brioche that appears in local bakeries in time for the yearly Twelfth Night celebration. It looks like gaudy technicolor coffee cake, iced in the Carnival colors of purple, green and gold (symbolizing justice, faith and power) and contains a prize hidden somewhere inside – a tiny plastic baby doll. When the cake is sliced and eaten, the lucky person who 'bites the baby' is cheered and feted. It also means that lucky person will buy the next celebratory cake.

Competing origin stories attribute the tradition to pre-Christian European tribes and randy French royalty, but the King cake is a modern Carnival tradition kept alive by the city's Mardi Gras krewes and loyal Louisiana confectionery fanatics. The exclusive Carnival societies – especially the Twelfth Night Revelers – used the King cake as a method of choosing each year's Mardi Gras symbolic 'royalty'. And the pastry zealots buy upwards of 750,000 cakes annually from local bakers. (These complex cakes are very rarely made in home kitchens.) Traditionally this ritual only took place on the Twelfth Night, but nowadays you'll find King cakes in office break rooms and school cafeterias throughout the Carnival season.

In earlier times, the featured prize would have been a dried bean, a gold coin, or a tiny porcelain figurine baked inside the cake. But today, the baby figurines are made of inexpensive molded plastic and inserted just before the cutting of the cake. Local bakeries used to 'hide the baby' as part of the icing process, but now leave that process up to the host – presumably to avoid lawsuits associated with the 'baby as potential choking hazard'.

Carnival season in New Orleans also means a flurry of smaller private celebrations and gatherings that precede parades, balls or other seasonal parties. Depending on the tone of the gathering, the foods can range from chill-chasing chicken **sauce piquante** to fancy hors d'oeuvre or delicate finger sandwiches filled with ham salad and cheesy artichoke dip.

In Acadiana, informal Carnival gatherings – including crawfish boils (see Crawfish in the Staples & Specialties chapter) and gumbo parties (see the Louisiana Gumbo Party chapter) – are yet another excuse for large-scale merriment and lively conversation.

Mardi Gras Day

The past days of cake gorging and parties have all been a precursor to today: Fat Tuesday, the culmination of the Carnival season. You're bumping shoulders with Zulu queens, Lady Godiva, Mardi Gras Indians in full plumage, masked and painted revelers, miles of marching bands and a large dancing rooster. There are strands of colored beads around your neck and your pockets are overflowing with doubloons (specially minted coins), insignia-stamped plastic cups and condoms. You have no idea what you are going to do with this stuff – except the condoms – but this is your proud booty of 'throws', tossed from the passing Carnival floats. Mardi Gras krewes with names like Momus, Zulu, Isis, Proteus, Bacchus and Tucks stage elaborate parades and throw doubloons and strings of plastic beads to crowds of eager spectators, who relentlessly scream the traditional plea of "Hey Mister! Throw me somethin'!" The streets are totally gridlocked with people and you are trying to maneuver through the crowd to engage in a little pre-Lenten overindulgence.

Imagine that you are a devout Catholic – perhaps you are – so today is your last day of dietary freedom before somber Lent begins on the morrow. It is time to run wild and feast before abstinence begins (sounds like a fore-runner to many modern diets). Giving up meat for Lent will mean no fleshy specialties for 40 days. Although the number of people partaking in Lenten vows may have dropped, the tradition of meat-feasting on Mardi Gras day continues, and tables – both private and commercial – are overflowing with New Orleans favorites like steak, ribs, roasts and baked hams. And, of course, drinks flow freely.

A store window display, New Orleans

In recent years, New Orleans' Mardi Gras celebration has become a victim of its own success. During the last weekend of the Carnival season, hoardes of tourists descend on the Crescent City, hellbent on drinking themselves into bare-chested oblivion. In what some call "the only sensible reaction to Mardi Gras," many locals abandon their homes and fly to Colorado's ski slopes until the party dies down.

Mardi Gras in the Cajun Prairie

In towns north of Lafayette, locals celebrate Mardi Gras a little differently. Instead of jostling for spoils to be thrown to them, the people here go out and get the spoils themselves. This is the **Courir de Mardi Gras** (Mardi Gras Run), for which grown men dress up and ride horses through the countryside, 'raiding' local homes and farms, procuring the requirements for a huge communal Mardi Gras gumbo. The Courir de Mardi Gras costumes have more of a rustic edge than the satin robes and feathered masks worn in the city. There's the **paillasse** (straw man) wearing a costume of straw, buttons and bits of metal, others wear **capuchons** (hoods) and masks. The original purpose of playfully 'stealing' these food items was a chance for the community to poke around people's farms to see if they had enough food left after the winter to last them through until the late spring. But nothing

comes to the rabble easily, chickens are set loose, sacks of rice are hidden, and pigs are greased so that they slip through the chasers' fingers.

Once the ingredients are caught, it's back to town for the communal cook up. Huge steaming cauldrons brimming with onions, chicken, pork and fragrant spices release their aromas through streets that jump with Cajun music and dancing.

Once the pot has been licked clean and the glamorous costumes have been reduced to rags, the locals – hung over and exhausted from glorious Carnival excess – are ready to face the somber season with mischievous and suitably depraved memories of another year's Mardi Gras.

Revelers at Mardi Gras, New Orleans

Jazz & Heritage Festival

After the unbridled chaos of Mardi Gras, New Orleans has a few weeks to prepare for the next big party – The New Orleans Jazz and Heritage Festival, the celebration of the city's music and culture. For two weekends from the end of April, this internationally renowned festival (known simply as JazzFest to locals) transforms the infield of the city's horse track (the Fairgrounds) into a nonstop flurry of amazing live music and an ideal spot to sample the diverse cuisines of the region.

Unlike most cultural festivals, where food booths are thrown in as an afterthought, JazzFest booth-holders enjoy a unique level of celebrity equal to the musical acts that grace the major stages. Diehard fans and repeat customers invariably have food factored into their festival routine. ("First, I go to that place that sells the crawfish-stuffed bread and send my son to get me a Mango Freeze, or three. Then I go sit in the gospel tent and let the voices just wash over me while I eat.")

Before you head to the Fairgrounds, prepare yourself by *not* filling up on a big breakfast. Arrive hungry and you can savor the plethora of foods available. Once you have made your way into the fair grounds – which won't be easy, given that you are milling around in a crowd of thousands – head straight for the food booths. April is crawfish season, so grab a crawfish pie for a mid-morning snack as you head

Drummer Freddy Staehle

over to the Food Heritage Stage. You might see an alligator-skinning demonstration, a session on how to make filé gumbo, or red beans and rice, or corn maque choux, or a tutorial on how to grow and use native fruits and vegetables, or maybe watch a New Orleans celebrity chef prepare a signature dish.

For lunch, head back to the booths, perhaps for a barbecued alligator poboy, then head for the seafood boil demonstration. Some happy Cajuns will take you step-by-step through a crawfish boil and at the end you might sample the spicy wares. The choice is staggering in this culinary wonderland.

Make your way to the tents for a late-afternoon musical interlude. The fair closes at 7pm, which leaves you just enough time to grab a small bowl of filé gumbo and to regret that you just can't fit in one more soft-shell crab poboy. But remember – there's always tomorrow.

Acme Oyster House, Iberville Street, New Orleans

SULTRY & SUGAR-DUSTED WELCOME TO JAZZFEST

It gets pretty hot in my hometown of Memphis. The heat can lead even a Baptist girl to do things she might not otherwise. But for as hot as Memphis gets, New Orleans gets hotter. It broils there, and one's mind and actions (and, in the end, one's reputation) meanders down unfamiliar streets. In New Orleans, one can never be sure where she'll end up.

A few years ago, my college roommate invited me to the JazzFest in New Orleans with a crew of her new post-college friends. New Orleans is about excess, and people come to New Orleans for two basic reasons: to drink an obscene amount of alcohol or to eat an obscene amount of food. Or, of course, for both, with some good jazz thrown in for ambiance.

Our room in the French Quarter was clean, airy, and way above our budget, but in line with the overindulgences of New Orleans.

Amber and I had lived together for 2½ years. She dated the boy who lived below us, David, who had become a close friend of mine in the process. I was thrilled, then, on our first night in New Orleans, when she asked me to be the maid of honor in their wedding, four years after their first kiss in our ramshackle apartment.

The next morning we met Amber's friends for breakfast. We sat at black wrought-iron tables on a little terrace off the hotel, drinking café au lait and eating pigs in a blanket (sausages wrapped in pastry). So civilized. Why everything changed once we left the hotel, I'll never be sure.

We loaded the shuttle to JazzFest, flag in tow. (We'd been warned of the crowds, and in a fit of good sense, bought one of those tacky nylon flags to stake our plot and serve as a beacon to those who get lost easily on drink runs.) We arrived around 10am, the heat beginning to make itself noticed as our thighs stuck to the vinyl seats of the bus. There were too many people for my taste. Too many armpits, too much sweat. But the music was loud and the food was good. This was no corn-dog heaven. Sure, you could get your basic funnel cake and foot-long (hotdogs) – so what? We were in New Orleans, and thanks be to God, the food followed suit: gigantic pots of red beans and rice, jambalaya, étouffée. Freshly fried calamari wrapped in sheets of newspaper, spritzed with fresh lemon halves. Handmade boudin. Just caught, just cooked, whole crawfish, still steaming from the boiling water and spices. Ice-cold beer to soothe the Louisiana heat. It all worked.

As the day wore on, each of us roamed the park in search of the perfect food to satisfy our 'All right! We're in New Orleans!' cravings. Having sat in the blaring sun for about five minutes longer than my tender, sunburned skin could bear, I began making my way toward the gospel tent. My nose took me on a detour to the crab stand, where I ordered the largest, most out-of-control sandwich I've eaten to this day: a soft-shell crab poboy. Sounds innocuous enough, I know. But picture a whole crab, deep-fried and set on freshly-baked French bread. Smear it with mayonnaise. Top it with shredded lettuce, sliced tomato, and pickles. Now sprinkle liberally with Louisiana Hot Sauce. This sandwich is a mess! Crab legs hanging out everywhere, lettuce sprouting out, tomatoes sliding past the bread when you take a bite. Now throw in a some foot-stomping, hand-clapping, soul-moving gospel singing in 87° heat with 97% humidity. So there I sat, protected from the sun by this giant tent, managing my poboy and listening to big black women filled with the Holy Spirit. Makes you want to believe in God. As the sun began to set, I headed back to our flag. There sat Amber, her friends, and a guy.

The guy's name was Jackson, from Kentucky, and Amber had met him at the boudin counter. He asked her for a napkin, and she invited him to our flag. When we headed back to our hotel that to shower for dinner, Jackson came along. He came with us too when we went to the oyster bar and slid countless oysters down our throats. Amber's fingers had slipped on a lemon wedge, and she'd lobbed it into another customer's lap, so Jackson appointed himself the official lemon spritzer. He prepared each of her oysters: dislodged the meat from its shell, spooned on a bit of cocktail sauce, and gave a hearty squeeze of lemon to mix with the liquor. Then he'd feed them to her.

Well, you know, Casanova fed his lovers oysters. And being fed oysters when you're slightly drunk from the heat . . . this is not appropriate behavior for a Baptist girl who is spoken for. I should have known what was going to happen. She should have known what was going to happen.

He, I'm quite sure, knew what was going to happen.

We finished up our dinner and wandered out into the cobblestone streets of the French Quarter. The whole Quarter is conducive to strolling: the architecture, wafts of good cooking, voodoo shops, titty bars, and drunk patrons always make for interesting conversation.

Six street musicians later, we stumbled upon Café du Monde, the most cliched place to visit in New Orleans. Clichés, though, have roots in the truth, and Café du Monde produces the most delectable beignets available. They're like doughnuts or sopapillas, only better. I don't know why they're better. In fact, I'm not even sure there is a difference. I just know that on a hot summer night in New Orleans, a beignet from Café du Monde melts on your tongue, powdered sugar goes everywhere, and café au lait adds the final dimension of flavors to your happy mouth.

Amber took a bite of her beignet. I noticed a patch of powdered sugar stayed on her cheek. Jackson did too. He brushed it off, then kissed her skin clean. The next week Amber broke off her engagement and moved to Kentucky.

I'll never know if it was the sultriness of the heat or the sultriness of the food, but that's how New Orleans is. It makes a girl do things she wouldn't normally do. It makes her go ways she never anticipated. And one can never, ever be sure where she'll end up.

Martha Hopkins

SMALL TOWN FAIRS & FESTIVALS

Louisiana's smaller towns seem to be in a constant state of celebration. From the coastal regions of Cajun Country to the piney hills and river bottoms of Northern Louisiana, even the tiniest communities dedicate annual festivals to local crops (such as corn, oysters, frogs or swine) or cultural traditions (railroads, fishing rodeos, or horse races). These events are usually clustered around the more temperate months of spring and fall. A local festival – be it a church fair, a Christmas festival or a competitive gumbo cook-off – can provide great opportunities to rub shoulders with the locals and explore the state's regional specialties.

The events are usually held during the same weekend each year (ie the last weekend in April for JazzFest) but check with local tourist offices for exact dates. You can also contact the Louisiana Association of Fairs & Festivals in Thibodaux for details on these and many other festivals.

February	La Grande Boucherie, Saint Martinville
March	Iowa Rabbit Festival, Iowa; Amite Oyster Festival and Rodeo, Amite
April	Ponchatoula Strawberry Festival, Ponchatoula; Boudin Festival, Broussard; *Le Festival de Étouffée*, Arnaudville; *Festival International de Louisiane*, Lafayette
May	Breaux Bridge Crawfish Festival, Breaux Bridge; Cochon de Lait (suckling pig) Festival, Mansura; Jambalaya Festival, Gonzales; Tunica-Biloxi Powwow, Marksville; Marion Mayhaw Festival, Marion
June	Louisiana Corn Festival, Bunkie; Smoked Meat Festival, Ville Platte; Louisiana Peach Festival, Ruston
July	Greater Mandeville Seafood Festival, Mandeville; Catfish Festival, Des Allemands
August	Delcambre Shrimp Festival, Delcambre
September	Frog Festival, Rayne; *Festival Acadiens*, Lafayette; Louisiana Sugarcane Festival, New Iberia
October	Andouille Festival, LaPlace; International Rice Festival, Crowley; Gumbo Festival, Chackbay; French Food Festival, Larose; Yambilee, Opelousas; St Martinville Pepper Festival, St Martinville
November	Giant Omelet Celebration, Abbeville; Cracklin Festival, Port Barre; Louisiana Pecan Festival, Colfax; Swine Festival, Basile
December	Christmas Festival, Natchitoches

The tuba pumps out the bass, New Orleans

Christmas Season

Even though snowstorms rarely drift this far south, natives of Louisiana take the Christmas season – and its rich edible traditions – very seriously. Let Bing Crosby croon over his beloved White Christmas, the holiday foods of Louisiana more than make up for flurries of fluffy flakes.

As with most communities that celebrate the holiday, Christmas is a time for appreciation of family, distant homecomings, constant celebration and special food. The first weeks of December are filled with parties at the office, parties with friends, and parties at home. Prickly fir trees are hauled indoors, covered with glittery ornaments and surrounded by gaily-wrapped gifts. Children are reluctantly wrestled into their Sunday clothes and mothers dress up for this characteristically formal season.

Each family has its own tradition, but tables are usually well stocked with rich and sweet foods that mark the holiday's indulgence. Sugar-dusted cookies (biscuits), sticky homemade candies, moist cakes, and special group cocktails (such as eggnog) make their yearly appearance. A gumbo made from the Thanksgiving turkey may be the centerpiece of a pre-Christmas meal, or perhaps a warming batch of oyster and artichoke soup. Baked hams and roast beef make perpetual snacking the norm. During the cold months of December and January, Gulf oysters are at their plumpest, so the versatile shellfish shows up on party tables as stew, soup, gumbo, and fancier starters including Oysters Rockefeller and Oysters Bienville (see Oysters in the Staples & Specialties chapter)

On Christmas Eve, a mixture of family and communal celebrations sweep the state. On the levees of Ascension Parish, huge bonfires burn atop the high river-bounding hills to guide Papá-Noel (Father Christmas) along the Mississippi River. In many houses, late-night gift exchanges and house-to-house visits culminate at Midnight Mass services to commemorate the birth of Jesus. In between this night of virtue and the following morning's chaotic 'Santa duties', a huge Christmas breakfast is served. The offerings will include: fluffy biscuits doused in sweet cane syrup or rich pain perdu ('lost bread', a baguette-based version of eggy French toast), with salty bacon or the New Orleans classic grits and grillades (see Brunch in The Culture of New Orleans chapter).

After a week of rest between major holidays, New Year's Eve arrives with its requisite midnight revelry and champagne toasts. Symbolic food traditions abound during New Year's Day, the most prevalent of which are the eating of tender black-eyed peas and cabbage – for good luck and plenty of cash in the new year. The usual starchy accompaniment to this tasty tradition is coarse-grained cornbread, which according to another tradition will ensure gold in one's purse in the coming year.

KEEPER OF THE NOG

My great Aunt Rose's annual Christmas Eve party was always a hit. Of all the celebrations on our extended family's Baton Rouge holiday circuit, it was the one that consistently achieved a perfect balance of chaos and civility. It was an event that struck the delicate equilibrium of holiday fancy dress and everyday informality. It was a gathering where adults felt comfortable in rapt conversation while packs of sugar-charged kids rocketed through the house, always seconds away from shattering shelves of porcelain bric-a-brac. For one night every year, Aunt Rose transformed her proper home into a very civilized seasonal circus – complete with long-suffering poodles, a burbling yellow lava lamp, and polished silver containers on every horizontal surface. Always the gracious hostess, Aunt Rose (the patron saint of other people's kids) presided over the crowd with a relaxed smile and a straight-from-the-beauty shop coif.

The whole affair was powered by her ethereal eggnog – the feather-light concoction that was ladled from an elaborate silver punch bowl into matching cups. Like the party itself, Rose's eggnog was a study in holiday paradox. In texture, it was between a fluffy chocolate mousse and liquid custard. The velvety mixture of eggs, heavy cream, extra-fine sugar and bourbon was both light as a cloud and mind-bendingly rich. Kids inhaled the nog because it closely resembled quaffable cake batter – sweet with vanilla and nutmeg. Adults upped the indulgence by innocently reaching for the cream pitcher conveniently topped with Jack Daniel's. "Just a little extra Christmas cheer," they'd say of their highly-flammable treat.

Rose Hebert Schatzle – 'Aunt Rose' to most – was everybody's favorite relative. In her youth, she was the brash bad girl who found good-natured trouble effortlessly. As my grandfather's sister, Rose had spent most of her life acting as confidante, guardian, and friend to my mother and her seven siblings. Perfectly pear-shaped and welcoming, Aunt Rose knew her role as aunt afforded her special privileges and her own set of rules. She was trusted by all and gently wielded a quasi-parental authority that didn't take itself too seriously. Aunt Rose was our family's middle ground – the comforting, forgiving connector between parents and children.

Later in life, she kept her reputation of 'feminine but fun', smelling of perfume and Winston cigars. In her tiny house, she tended her poodles (Mim, Bay, and Petite Chou) and developed a talent for spoiling other people's kids. Her kitchen cabinets always held stashes of chocolate milk and condensed milk, and she could sidestep our parent's dietary taboos with a wave of her hand. On every trip to Baton Rouge, we'd stop in for a visit, while Mama and Rose would talk over coffee. "Carmelite," she'd say in between poodle yaps, "always keep your life on a cash basis."

For some reason, our family always arrived early to Rose's Christmas party to help with the preparations. While Rose busied herself with pans of buttered pecans, I'd watch my mother and her sister Madeline crack, and painstakingly separate, dozens of eggs for the upcoming nog. The egg whites went into the mixer until they turned to weightless foam, then the yolks went in with sugar 'until it all looks lemony'. A generous slug of bourbon helped to 'cook the yolks a bit', and then the delicate hand-folding process began. My mother would take a little bit of the fluffy egg foam and gently blend it into the bright yellow mix of liquor and yolk. A little more, and the mixture started to inflate and smell like Christmas. A few more turns of the spatula, and it was ready to go into the shiny punchbowl with spoons for the truly dainty.

A few hours later, everyone was back in holiday attire and the party was in full swing. And as usual, everybody felt perfectly at home despite the confines of the dreaded church clothes. Rose's tree twinkled next to the lava lamp, and the elaborately-wrapped presents reflected the amorphous light. Rose's girls would flit around checking the ham, rinsing the cups, and corralling the kids as the need arose. And above it all, Aunt Rose would smile – the happy conductor of her chaotic Christmas chorus.

Aunt Rose's Eggnog

Ingredients

12	eggs
12 tblsp	powdered sugar (plus 4 more for egg whites)
½ pint	whipping cream
1 tblsp	vanilla extract (or more to taste)
4 fl oz	bourbon (or more to taste)
	freshly ground nutmeg

Separate eggs, putting yolks in one bowls and whites in another. (Separate the whites in a small bowl before adding them to the large bowl. This way if you get a yolk in the white, you only lose one egg white. The smallest amount of yolk will mess up the egg whites!)

Beat the yolks and 12 tablespoons of powdered sugar until thick and lemony. Add bourbon to 'cook' the yolks. Set aside.

Making sure your beaters are clean, add a dash of salt to the liquid egg whites and beat until the whites are very stiff – almost dry. Carefully add more powdered sugar (about 4 tablespoons) to sweeten the whites.

In a separate bowl, beat the whipping cream with a little powdered sugar (about ¼ to ½ cup). Now you've got whipped cream.

Carefully combine the whipped cream, yolks, egg whites, and vanilla in a punch bowl. Add the beaten egg whites last, folding them into the cream and egg yolk mixture. Sprinkle nutmeg over each serving and have extra bourbon available for those who prefer more grog in their nog.

Serves 12

St Patrick's Day

Since their mass arrival in the mid 1800s, the Irish have played an important part in shaping New Orleans as we know it today. During the exodus that followed the Irish Potato Famine they formed strong communities in the areas bounding either side of the French Quarter – the Irish Channel (part of the lower Garden District) and the downriver district known as the Ninth Ward.

Many labored to build the channels that prevented the city from flooding, and Irish surnames figure in the history of the city's founding fathers. So, in a city looking for any excuse to revel, an event celebrating Ireland's patron saint is not to be missed.

Keeping with the local tradition of 'parade throws', floats in St Patrick's Day parades fling edible treats to cheering onlookers instead of the usual baubles and beads. Mardi Gras doubloons and other gaudy throws are replaced by cabbages, onions, potatoes and carrots, the primary ingredients that make up a traditional Irish stew. It's a tradition that makes for a distinctly high-impact experience, so when the city goes green you'd better be agile or wear a protective helmet.

The crowds follow the parade from the French Quarter into the Irish Channel. Along the way the participants make regular stops at various bars to enjoy that most American (and disgusting) of St Patrick's Day specialties, beer dyed green with liquid food coloring. Not the most flavorful of traditions, but in the end, a party's a party.

Musicians busking outside a street cafe, New Orleans

The Feast of St Joseph

Two days after the Irish celebrate their favorite saint, the Sicilian community honors their patron, St Joseph, with feasts and elaborate rituals every March 19th. St Joseph is the patron saint of the poor, the widowed, unwed mothers and carpenters, and is much loved by Sicilians. He is credited with saving the Sicilians from famine in the Middle Ages, and they have been grateful ever since. Elaborate food-laden altars are prepared to thank St Joseph for favors granted in the past year and to acknowledge that food should not be taken for granted. The poor and destitute are always invited to partake in the feasts and surplus food is distributed to the needy.

To participate in the celebration, buy a copy of the newspaper – the *New Orleans Times-Picayune* – and find a listing of churches holding St Joseph's services. When you enter the church you'll find a large altar heaving with food – biscuits, bread and fig cakes – all shaped into crosses, crown of thorns, sacred hearts, palm leaves, chalices and St Joseph's staff. Special fried pastries called **pignolatti** are shaped like the pine cones that Jesus allegedly used as childhood toys. There will also be fish, shrimp, stuffed peppers, stuffed eggplant, stuffed squash, oysters, **pasta milanese** (made with anchovy, wild anise, pine nuts, currants and dusted with bread crumbs to symbolize the carpenter Joseph's sawdust), vegetable fritters, stuffed artichokes and mountains of fresh fruit all interspersed with statuary of the Saint himself, his holy family and plenty of candles. Hungry? Well, you'll have to wait, because mass comes before feasting. Once mass has been finished, there will be a knock on the door and someone will ask who is there.

"Jesus, Mary and Joseph," comes the reply.

"What do you want?"

"We seek food and shelter."

"Go away, there is no room for you here!"

The request and response are repeated twice more. At the third time of asking, the holy family and a group of saints (a group of children wearing old sheets) are admitted into the church's sanctuary. The holy family and retinue are fed with food from the altar and their plates are continually replenished as a re-enactment of the miracle of the loaves and fishes. When the little holy family have had their fill, the salivating congregation cheers "Viva San Giuseppe!" and the communal feasting begins. Help yourself to the culinary bounty and don't forget to place a monetary gracias to St Joseph in one of the receptacles on the altar. As you leave you will be handed a small bag containing some holy bread, a St Joseph medal and some fava beans.

That evening, at the parade in the French Quarter, fava beans will be thrown into the crowd to symbolize the time St Joseph saved the Sicilians from famine by saving the fava bean crops. Fava is considered a lucky bean and it's said that if you carry one in your purse it will never be empty.

Fais Do Do

The social celebrations of the Cajuns don't stop at the communal table – oftentimes there's also dancing to be done afterwards. Originally referring to any organized Cajun dance (be it at home or in the community) the term fais do do now refers mainly to outdoor street dances that take place during local festivals.

The somewhat fanciful name comes from the French sweet nothings that mothers whisper to their babies to send them off to sleep. (Cajun mothers sometimes soothe their children with coos of "do do, baby. Do do.") During the house dances that were common in earlier times, mothers would coo their children to sleep in a quiet room attached to the dancehall. Once the last *bebe* had dropped off to sleep, the adults danced the night away.

Live music at Prajean's, Lafayette

Like its food, Cajun music is an invigorating blend of hearty ingredients, and when you arrive for a fais do do, don't expect to sit on the sidelines and watch. Everybody – whatever their condition – dances to the irresistible rhythms of fiddles and accordions et al. The basic Cajun step is a flowing partner dance with waltz, two-step and more complex jitterbug variations. The dancing traditionally begins after dinner and replenishment is usually required by midnight. During the interlude, you might dig into a chicken gumbo, rich beef stew cooked with plenty of onions and thyme, links of boudin, and another beer to cool your sweat. Whatever your snack, you'll quickly burn it off as it's immediately back to intoxicating the spirit with dance. If the fais do do reaches morning light, you can look forward to strong coffee, cake and sugar cookies.

The Cajun Boucherie

If you're squeamish about slaughter and prefer not to see your food in *extremely* raw form, you'd better miss the early stages of the traditional Acadian boucherie (communal pig butchering). Once a critical part of any Cajun community's culinary life, the boucherie is now less of a family affair than a large-scale festival celebrating the noble pig and its contribution to Louisiana cuisine. The most well known celebration (La Grande Boucherie) is held every February in the small Acadiana town of St Martinville. (For more details on the specialties listed in this section, see Pork in the Staples & Specialties chapter.)

In the early morning hours, a pig is killed; its throat slit and the blood caught in a basin, to be used in the production of boudin rouge (red boudin; pork blood sausage). Since boudin rouge cannot be sold commercially due to health regulations, a boucherie may be the only place where you can enjoy this Cajun specialty.

Next, the pig is split, scraped, skinned, and the fatty hide is rendered in black-iron cauldrons over open fires to make **cracklins** (known as **gratons** in local Cajun French dialect; see the boxed text Cracklin Man in the Staples & Specialties chapter). Much early-morning beer drinking accompanies this bloody work – both for the workers and onlookers.

The carcass is then hoisted up onto a table and butchered into its various components. The head, shoulders and feet are placed in a pot to cook all day for **hog's head cheese** (a chunky, gelatinous sausage made from the meat of the pig's head). The backbone is made into a stew called **reintier de cochon**, the ribs are used for the barbecue, and all the remaining meat is ground up to make the various specialty sausages, including boudin blanc, boudin rouge, and andouille.

Before the advent of refrigeration, boucheries were regular events during the cooler months in Southern Louisiana. As the fresh meat could not be kept for too long, families would gather together to slaughter a hog, prepare the meat and divide it up among themselves. The following week, another family's pig would be slaughtered and the whole bloody process would begin again.

It takes all day to slaughter and prepare the animal but a boucherie is traditionally a family event and everybody pitches in – preparing seasonings, piping filling into the clean sausage casings, playing music and cooking the cracklins. The day traditionally ends with a plate of backbone stew, some fresh boudin, music and an informal fais do do. The modern variation of the boucherie resembles the other cultural festivals of the area, where most of the spectators show up to eat, dance, and toast a few beers to their friend the pig.

Pulling boudin from the pot, Lafayette

DEEP-FRIED TURKEY

Just as the crawfish boiling rigs (see Special Utensils in the Home Cooking & Traditions chapter) represent the oilfield's contribution to Cajun cuisine, the invention of the deep-fried turkey is Louisiana's nod to the American Thanksgiving tradition.

Although it sounds awfully complicated, the process is very simple – if you own a high-output propane burner and a 15-gallon pot, that is. The outdoor cooking process is quick, efficient, and borders on performance art. It's also another chance for Cajun men to show off their prodigious (and often unconventional) cooking skills.

The standard oversized crawfish pot is filled with vegetable oil and heated to a scorching 375°F (190.5°C). While the oil is heating on the roaring flame, the turkey is injected with pepper sauce (thanks to a menacing oversized syringe) and rubbed on the outside with a standard Cajun spice mixture. When the oil reaches the magic temperature, the huge bird is carefully lowered into the blistering fat, where it cooks to a deep golden brown. After about 20-30 minutes, the carcass is lifted from the oil, drained, and carved.

If you've never tried the normally bland bird cooked this way, you wouldn't even recognize it as the American Thanksgiving standard. The meat is moist and flavorful (with an added zing from the injected marinade) without the slightest trace of oil. The skin is crispy and spicy with a little caramelized sweetness. And when the celebratory autumn meal has ended, the well-browned bones make a beautiful stock for the traditional Cajun post-Thanksgiving treat, turkey bone gumbo.

This novel treatment has spread across the US in recent years, inspiring home chefs to invest in big burners and pots for the cooking of the traditional banquet bird. Like most of the Cajun foodways, it's a generous (and delicious) gift from Louisiana's Acadians to the world.

regional
variations

Encompassing everything from cosmopolitan quarters to backwater bayous, the diverse terrain of Louisiana is home to an equally diverse collection of cuisines. And although New Orleans harbors all the flavors of the state, the best places to taste regional specialties are often outside the city's borders.

New Orleans & Surrounds

In New Orleans, there are restaurants competing for your appetite on almost every corner, and there's never a shortage of good food. Ironically, it has been New Orleans' inability to grow much food that has contributed to its culinary diversity. As a port city with average elevation of two feet *below* sea level, it has always been better suited to river trade than agriculture. Produce came downriver to the port, and key ingredients and influences arrived from Europe and the Caribbean. By connecting the Mississippi River to the world, New Orleans became a powerful shipping center and the cradle of Creole cuisine.

This importation of flavors continues to be a celebrated characteristic of the city's cuisine, and many local chefs have made their names by adapting cooking techniques and ingredients.

In this section, we outline the distinctions between some New Orleans' neighborhoods; for information on the different restaurants, and a map to guide you to the best, see the Where to Eat & Drink chapter.

French Quarter

The historic French Quarter is the hub of New Orleans' bustling tourist trade and home to well-established restaurant favorites and contemporary upstarts alike. Within the French Quarter you'll find traditional bastions like 150-year-old Antoine's, the oldest restaurant in town, as well as the thoroughly nuevo NOLA, chef Emeril Lagasse's second outpost of New New Orleans Cuisine.

Around any corner, you'll find historic Creole establishments serving decadent **Eggs Sardou** (poached eggs with artichoke and spinach topped with Hollandaise sauce) or secluded barrooms that haven't seen the light of day since they opened sometime in the 18th century.

The Quarter is home to the distinctive muffuletta and the best place to get your round-the-clock beignet fix. Unlike many designated tourist districts that are all flash and no substance, the Quarter is still popular with local foodies. The only *real* time they avoid dining in the area is during Carnival, but more about that in the Celebrating with Food chapter.

3am in Bourbon Street, New Orleans

REGIONAL VARIATIONS

REGIONAL VARIATIONS

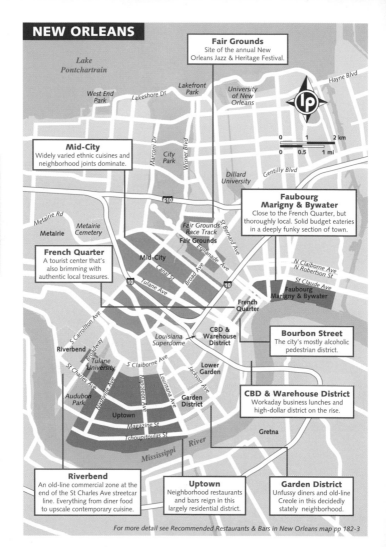

NEW ORLEANS

Fair Grounds
Site of the annual New Orleans Jazz & Heritage Festival.

Lake Pontchartrain

West End Park

Lakeshore Dr

Lakefront Park

University of New Orleans

Hayne Blvd

Mid-City
Widely varied ethnic cuisines and neighborhood joints dominate.

Marconi Dr

City Park

Wisner Blvd

Dillard University

Gentilly Blvd

Faubourg Marigny & Bywater
Close to the French Quarter, but thoroughly local. Solid budget eateries in a deeply funky section of town.

Metairie Rd

Metairie Cemetery

Metairie

610

Fair Grounds Race Track

Fair Grounds

St Bernard Ave

N Claiborne Ave
N Robertson St

St Claude Ave

Faubourg Marigny & Bywater

French Quarter
A tourist center that's also brimming with authentic local treasures.

Mid-City

Canal St

10

Tulane Ave

Esplanade Ave

Broad Ave

French Quarter

S Carrollton Ave

Broadway

Riverbend

Tulane University

Louisiana Superdome

S Claiborne Ave

CBD & Warehouse District

Lower Garden

Jackson Ave

Bourbon Street
The city's mostly alcoholic pedestrian district.

CBD & Warehouse District
Workaday business lunches and high-dollar district on the rise.

St Charles Ave

Napoleon Ave

Louisiana Ave

Garden District

Gretna

Audubon Park

Nashville Ave

Uptown

Magazine St

Tchoupitoulas St

River

Mississippi

Riverbend
An old-line commercial zone at the end of the St Charles Ave streetcar line. Everything from diner food to upscale contemporary cuisine.

Uptown
Neighborhood restaurants and bars reign in this largely residential district.

Garden District
Unfussy diners and old-line Creole in this decidedly stately neighborhood.

0   1   2 km
0   0.5   1 mi

For more detail see Recommended Restaurants & Bars in New Orleans map pp 182-3

CBD & Warehouse District

Lying between the Superdome and the Mississippi, these two commercial districts also contain some solid workaday examples of New Orleans food. Starch-shirt lawyers and other downtown workers crowd the many reasonably priced lunch joints for a midday refueling, while classic 'businessman's lunch' establishments also do a brisk trade. Poboys are a great bet here, with coma-inducing overstuffed **shrimp loaves** or gravy-drenched **debris** being popular options. The newly-swankified Warehouse district is home to a host of art galleries and high-dollar restaurants.

Uptown & Riverbend

Thanks to the picturesque St Charles Avenue streetcar line, Uptown is another popular destination for hungry city center travelers. This is the neighborhood for trying experimental Creole cuisine at Jacques-Imo's, all-you-can-eat chicken and red beans at Dunbar's, or cooling sugary goodness at Plum Street Snowballs (see New Orleans Restaurants in the Where to Eat & Drink chapter).

REGIONAL VARIATIONS

DON'T MISS

- A frosty schooner of Abita beer and fried green tomatoes at Liuzza's.
- The obligatory café au lait and piping hot beignets at Café du Monde.
- A dozen raw oysters chased with a cold beer at any of the city's famed oyster bars.
- A debris poboy filled with roast beef cooked to its tender disintegration point, then soaked in gravy at Mother's.
- Fabulous crusty French bread.
- Soft-shell crabs during the spring-summer season.
- Crispy fried catfish in Des Allemands.
- An after-dinner stroll through the gas-lit streets of the French Quarter.

Mid-City

This bustling but largely untouristed zone has a selection of the city's best Vietnamese restaurants and two of the classic New Orleans' neighborhood restaurants – Mandina's and Liuzza's (see New Orleans Restaurants in the Where to Eat & Drink chapter).

A little exploration into other neighborhoods – the Faubourg Marigny, the Bywater, Garden District, and Magazine Street – can yield exceptional eating as well. Just keep your ears open and, when possible, get advice from a well-fed local (there is no other kind). But wherever you find yourself, rest assured that outstanding experiences far outnumber the duds. Terrific restaurants have sprung up around the Fair Grounds, and it is worth exploring these parts even when the Jazz & Heritage Festival isn't on.

New Orleans skyline

Around New Orleans

New Orleans may be the culinary epicenter of the region, however this doesn't mean that the choice or quality of food decreases the farther you stray from the French Quarter. Take time out from the tourist haunts and venture on a culinary day-trip, perhaps north for a microbrewery tour, or west toward the Cajun heartland. Which ever direction you choose, you won't go hungry.

If you head southeast, down the Bayou Terre-aux-Boeufs, you'll find yourself standing on creaky wooden docks watching boats bring in their haul of shrimp, crab and fish. Unlike with the bigger boats working the Gulf, the catch here will invariably end up on local tables and in New Orleans rather than in processing factories. This area is also very popular with recreational fishermen, so if casting a line appeals to you, this is a fine place to do it.

The lakeside suburb of Bucktown is home to a small fleet of boats that haul in their catch from Lake Pontchartrain. Here you can sample fresh shrimp sold from outdoor vendors. A short drive north of New Orleans across the Pontchartrain Bridge will bring you to Abita Springs. Once popular due to the curative properties of its water, Abita Springs now has the honor of being home to a burgeoning microbrewery (see the boxed text in the Drinks of New Orleans chapter).

Driving west from New Orleans will lead you to Des Allemands, so named for the German immigrants who settled and planted wheat here. Des Allemands is now on the very outskirts of suburban New Orleans and, while no more wheat is grown here, there is a thriving catfish industry. If you visit Des Allemands on the first weekend in July you can attend the annual Catfish Festival. If you visit at any other time, you can still try the local specialty, catfish battered in cornmeal and deep fried.

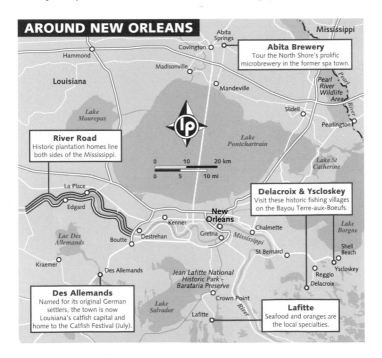

AROUND NEW ORLEANS

Abita Brewery
Tour the North Shore's prolific microbrewery in the former spa town.

River Road
Historic plantation homes line both sides of the Mississippi.

Delacroix & Yscloskey
Visit these historic fishing villages on the Bayou Terre-aux-Boeufs.

Des Allemands
Named for its original German settlers, the town is now Louisiana's catfish capital and home to the Catfish Festival (July).

Lafitte
Seafood and oranges are the local specialties.

Mississippi · Abita Springs · Covington · Hammond · Madisonville · Louisiana · Mandeville · Pearl River Wildlife Area · Lake Maurepas · Slidell · Pearlington · Lake Pontchartrain · Lake St Catherine · La Place · Edgard · Kenner · New Orleans · Chalmette · Lake Borgne · Lac Des Allemands · Boutte · Destrehan · Gretna · Mississippi · St Bernard · Shell Beach · Kraemer · Des Allemands · Jean Lafitte National Historic Park - Barataria Preserve · Reggio · Yscloskey · Delacroix · Lake Salvador · Crown Point · River · Lafitte

0 10 20 km
0 5 10 mi

Cajun Country

If New Orleans is the largest French city in the US, then Acadiana – Cajun Country – is its rural counterpart. Though the area shares a common French heritage with New Orleans, Acadiana lives its own brand of French frontier culture, marked by a unique history, cuisine and dialect. Many cultural elements commonly associated with New Orleans – hard-driving accordion music, spicy boiled crawfish and a host of rustic, flavorsome dishes – are actually products of this wild and watery section of the state.

The region itself stretches from the marshlands of Louisiana's south central coast, north through the broad coastal prairies and ends in the

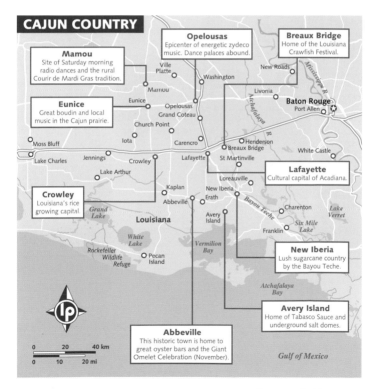

CAJUN COUNTRY

Opelousas
Epicenter of energetic zydeco music. Dance palaces abound.

Breaux Bridge
Home of the Louisiana Crawfish Festival.

Mamou
Site of Saturday morning radio dances and the rural Courir de Mardi Gras tradition.

Eunice
Great boudin and local music in the Cajun prairie.

Crowley
Louisiana's rice growing capital.

Lafayette
Cultural capital of Acadiana.

New Iberia
Lush sugarcane country by the Bayou Teche.

Avery Island
Home of Tabasco Sauce and underground salt domes.

Abbeville
This historic town is home to great oyster bars and the Giant Omelette Celebration (November).

Ville Platte, Washington, New Roads, Mississippi R., Mamou, Livonia, Eunice, Opelousas, Baton Rouge, Port Allen, Grand Coteau, Atchafalaya, Church Point, Iota, Carencro, Henderson, Breaux Bridge, White Castle, Moss Bluff, Lake Charles, Jennings, Crowley, Lafayette, St Martinville, Lake Arthur, Kaplan, Loreauville, New Iberia, Abbeville, Erath, Bayou Teche, Charenton, Lake Verret, Avery Island, Six Mile Lake, Franklin, Grand Lake, Louisiana, White Lake, Vermilion Bay, Rockefeller Wildlife Refuge, Pecan Island, Atchafalaya Bay, Gulf of Mexico

0   20   40 km
0   10   20 mi

Sunset on a Louisiana swamp

Outside Rocky and Lisa's Bayou Boudin

rolling hills around the state's narrow waistline. It was in this area that refugees from the French Canadian province of Acadie settled, mainly along the coastline of the Gulf of Mexico and the slow-moving brown bayous that curve through Acadiana's prolific wetlands.

The topography of the land – where saltwater meets fresh – is home to an amazingly diverse range of wildlife, all of which became fodder for Cajun food culture. The Gulf and the freshwater network of slow-moving rivers teemed with countless types of fish, crustaceans and shellfish, including crabs, oysters and Acadiana's sacred edible totem, the crawfish (see Crawfish in the Staples & Specialties chapter). The semisolid, brackish marshlands were also home to wild ducks and boar. The open prairie proved to be perfect for raising cattle and cultivating rice, in addition to providing habitats for innumerable bird species – the perfect marriage of food on the hoof, from the land, and on the wing.

MEN IN THE KITCHEN

Anyone who believes that 'a woman's place is in the kitchen' hasn't stepped up to a Louisiana stove. Cooking in Acadiana transcends gender lines and is as likely to be carried out by men as women. Louisiana men enjoy good reputations as cooks and have been known to brag as much about their personal gumbo recipe as their adeptness with a hunting rifle. They are also likely to cook large-scale specialty dishes (boiled crawfish, jambalaya for 50) that require hefty kitchen equipment such as butane-powered burners and oversized pots. In a Cajun kitchen, *everybody* cooks (see the Home Cooking & Traditions chapter).

Cajun History

Largely unsettled by Europeans until the late 1700s, southwest Louisiana became home to French refugees from the Canadian maritime province of Acadie (the French colonial name for modern-day Nova Scotia).

Forcibly expelled from their homes by conquering British troops in 1755, the exiled Acadians wandered in a boat-bound diaspora known as the Grand Derangement. After years of exile, the first Acadians arrived in Louisiana around 1763. Ironically they came as guests of the ruling Spanish Colonial government, who offered them farms in the less-populated territories west of New Orleans. The initial land grants the Acadians received were along the bayous and other waterways, but the Acadians (now referred to as Cajuns) spread throughout the region, content to rebuild their communities in relative isolation.

In their new home of Acadiana, the Cajuns adapted the same fishing and survival skills that served them well in Acadie, and flourished until well into the 20th century. Again, the group was left to its own devices and maintained their traditional ways and Cajun French language – a unique dialect based on archaic French – until oil (and later food culture) was discovered in the 20th century.

The Family Table

With strong connections to both family and land, Cajun culture expresses these ties most strongly at the table. The lands of Southern Louisiana provided an ample bounty of raw materials, which the Acadians-turned-Cajuns adapted into their trademark cuisine. The frontier survival experience mixed with the thoroughly Gallic 'eat everything' tradition to create a style of cookery unique to the Louisiana landscape.

The settlers adapted their cooking styles to incorporate the freshest, most plentiful ingredients around. Bayou Cajuns pulled freshwater fish from the murky brown streams while coastal communities cast their nets into the Gulf's shallow, salty waters. Farther upland, the prairie Cajuns made gumbos from their most abundant resources – barnyard staples like chicken and pork (see Gumbo in the Staples & Specialties chapter). Household gardens provided fresh vegetables and spices well-suited to the native climate, such as sweet potatoes, peppers, tomatoes. Styles varied from town to town, but the common spicing and cooking techniques united these variations into a coherent cuisine that's more rough around the edges than the smoother, more refined Creole cooking of New Orleans. The trademark dishes of Cajun cuisine – jambalaya, boiled crawfish, and certain gumbos – are solid one-dish meals designed to feed the masses (and their friends) at a moment's notice.

Acadiana Eating Tour

In the cities and smaller towns of Cajun Louisiana, restaurants are extensions of the family table, and as a result it's damn near impossible to buy bad food. This is culinary Darwinism at its finest: if it doesn't taste good, it doesn't survive. It's that simple.

The fame of the region is built on fresh seafood, with different towns renowned for local specialties. For example, a Cajun in the 'Cajun capital' of Lafayette will gladly drive 20 minutes to the oyster houses of Abbeville if craving the salty shellfish, and another 20 to the shrimp docks in Delcambre for the catch of the day.

Every community celebrates some kind of natural harvest, be it animal, vegetable, or mineral, during an annual free-for-all festival. Street dances and huge feasts mark the Crawfish Festival in Breaux Bridge, the Frog Festival in Rayne, and New Iberia's Sugarcane Festival. At any time of year, you're never too far from a celebration or a spiritual, full-contact eating experience (see the boxed text Fairs & Festivals in the Celebrating with Food Chapter).

REGIONAL VARIATIONS

DON'T MISS

- The home of Tabasco and numerous bird sanctuaries on Avery Island.
- The freshest Gulf oysters in the historic town of Abbeville.
- Boiling points for a meal of seafood that's fresh from the net .
- Small-town meat markets where you can buy freshly made boudin.
- *Rendez-vous des Cajuns,* a Saturday night Cajun radio program that is broadcast from the renovated Liberty Theatre in Eunice. Host Barry Jean Ancelet, a folklorist at Lafayette's University of Louisiana, regularly gives out recipes, although they may be in French.
- The many food-based fairs and festivals that are held throughout the year (see Fairs & Festivals in the Celebrating with Food chapter).
- A scenic drive through the fertile sugarcane fields around New Iberia.

The Acme Oyster House, New Orleans

JUST ANOTHER FISH FRY

"Jeff's frying fish tonight. You want to come by for dinner?"

Every time I visit my family in Baton Rouge, I hope for an invitation like this. On hot summer nights, my sister Charlotte can occasionally convince her husband Jeff to have an outdoor fish fry. Part of it is for convenience – cooking outside makes for a cooler house – but the other part is for pure taste. Besides being a classic Louisiana fisherman, Jeff can fry his catch better than any human alive.

Raised in Baton Rouge, Jeff makes his living at a local petrochemical plant, but his real calling is in the fishing camps and duck blinds of the Sportsman's Paradise. Since he was a boy, Jeff has fished Louisiana's rivers, bayous, and bays almost constantly. Whatever the time of year, he finds some way to get out on the water in search of speckled trout, bluegill, freshwater bass, snapper, drum and goggle-eye. And in true sportsman's form, when he's not fishing, he's plotting hunting expeditions to his duck camp.

Whenever Jeff comes home from a fishing trip, he meticulously cleans the boat, stows his tackle and unpacks plastic bags of freshly skinned fillets. Sometimes they go into the freezer for later, but on lucky days – like today– they're cooked within a day of the catch.

On this particular night, Jeff unpacks his huge propane burner and sets up an oversized cast-iron pot on the burner's stand. With the click a lighter and howl of jet-propelled flame, the pot (filled with vegetable oil) starts adding more heat to the evening air. As the oil hots up, Jeff rinses  and dries the fillets before dredging them in a seasoned mixture of cornmeal and flour. He then delicately floats the slabs of trout in the blistering oil. His sons Daniel and Philip, even at the active ages of four and six, know to stay back during this part of the process.

Minutes later, the fillets float to the surface of the oil, bubbling, sizzling and golden brown. With one quick motion, Jeff picks the fillets out of the grease and adds three more to the pot. Before long, the platter of freshly fried fish is heavy and hot – and we go inside for dinner. As we begin munching through the perfectly cooked strips of tender fish, six-year-old Philip turns to tell me about his memorable trips on his daddy's boat. I try to listen, but in the end I'm a bit distracted. Even as my nephew recounts the story of his big fishing trip, I'm lost in the crunch and amazing flavors of what that family considers "just another fish fry".

Pableaux Johnson

Hunting & Fishing

Living in a state nicknamed 'The Sportsman's Paradise' it's only natural that the denizens of Cajun Louisiana have developed active hunting and fishing cultures. Every family has at least one member who lives to head out to the state's wilderness areas, eager to engage in the 'harvesting' of unfarmed foodstuffs.

Groups of local men live for the different seasons of the sportsman's year – duck, deer, and fishing among them. The tradition of visiting a stripped-down summer house can either be for a fishing camp on the coastal waterways or a deer lease somewhere where the skittish animals roam free. Driving through any residential area, you're likely to see aluminum fishing boats on trailers and restless hunting dogs awaiting the next trip to the lease.

Not surprisingly, these outdoor activities also have an important social function. Hunkering down in a marshy duck blind or shooting a buck is a common right of passage for Louisiana boys. Hunters and fisherfolk also constitute an important voice for wildlife and environmental conservation in the state. It is through these activities that the traditional ties to – and respect for – the land are maintained in modern times.

The bounty of the hunt almost always becomes the featured dish at the next gumbo party or family fish fry. Refrigerators throughout the region are usually filled with frozen bags of fish fillets, cleaned ducks or deer steaks waiting their turn on the table. Locals joke that in Louisiana, there's no such thing as 'extra freezer space'.

REGIONAL VARIATIONS

Shrimp jambalaya, Livonia

Northern Louisiana

With few French cultural roots to speak of, Northern Louisiana is the only part of the state that can be properly described as 'The Deep South'. From the northwest's piney hills to Mississippi delta farmland, this section of the state was traditionally populated by the farmers of British extraction who worked their way westward with the expanding American frontier. The locals tend to be Protestant (Baptist, Methodist, and Presbyterian), which results in a social conservatism and linguistic drawl that this region shares with its bordering states of Mississippi, east Texas, and Arkansas.

Although Natchitoches was the first permanent settlement in Louisiana – a fort was built there in 1741 – development was slow to come to this

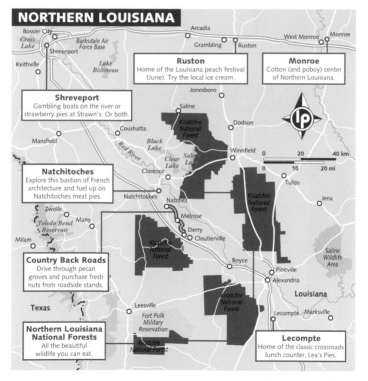

NORTHERN LOUISIANA

Ruston
Home of the Louisiana peach festival (June). Try the local ice cream.

Monroe
Cotton (and poboy) center of Northern Louisiana.

Shreveport
Gambling boats on the river or strawberry pies at Strawn's. Or both.

Natchitoches
Explore this bastion of French architecture and fuel up on Natchitoches meat pies.

Country Back Roads
Drive through pecan groves and purchase fresh nuts from roadside stands.

Northern Louisiana National Forests
All the beautiful wildlife you can eat.

Lecompte
Home of the classic crossroads lunch counter, Lea's Pies.

James Laysonne and his meat pies, Natchitoches

part of the state. The northern section of the state didn't really open up until the Louisiana Purchase, when Americans seeking new opportunities began to investigate and develop this region.

The first railroad into Northern Louisiana connected the river city of Shreveport to Dallas, and the area around the town has always had stronger connections with the 'Bible Belt' states of Texas and Arkansas than with heavily French-Catholic Southern Louisiana. The adjoining corners of Texas, northwest Louisiana and Arkansas are considered one cultural/economic area and go under the common name of ArkLaTex. Monroe, on the eastern side of the region, is a trading center for surrounding cotton farms in the region.

The major industries in the North are oil, cotton, lumber and natural gas. The area is known for its wildlife preserves, especially the sprawling Kisatchie National Forest, which are full of beautiful (and edible) wild game and freshwater fish. Much like in Cajun Country, hunting and fishing are the most popular pastime activities since deer, rabbit, squirrel, duck, dove, catfish, bass, bream and even bullfrogs are so plentiful.

Turnip Greens

A common vegetable option on Soul Food menus, turnip greens are cheap and plentiful throughout Northern Louisiana. This recipe conforms to the country-style method of cooking vegetables – cook the hell out of them and make 'em sweet.

Ingredients

6 bunches	turnip greens	4 slices	bacon
2 tsp	oil	2 tblsp	sugar
½ tsp	salt	½ tsp	freshly ground
½ cup	water		black pepper

Pick the leaves from the stems of the turnip greens and wash the leaves well in salted water. You will probably need to change the water three times to get every last bit of grit out.

Cook the bacon in the oil over low heat in a heavy-based pot until the bacon is translucent. Add the greens to the pot.

Mix the bacon through the greens thoroughly. Add the sugar, salt, pepper and water.

Simmer over a very low heat for 3 hours. Check occasionally – you may need to add a small amount of water if the greens start to stick to the bottom of the pot. Serve hot.

Serves 6

Natchitoches Meat Pie

Co-author Charmaine O'Brien was able to obtain this recipe from Gay Melder of Natchitoches.

Pie filling		**Crust**	
1 tsp	shortening	25oz (700g)	plain flour
1lb (450g)	ground pork	2 tsp	salt
1lb (450g)	ground beef	1 tsp	baking soda
1 bunch	green onions, chopped	½ cup	shortening
1 clove	garlic, minced	2	eggs
1	bell pepper, chopped	1 cup	milk
1 tblsp	flour		oil for deep frying
	salt and pepper		

Crust
Sift together the dry ingredients and cut in the shortening. Beat the eggs and add to the milk. Stir into the dry ingredients and work until the dough holds together enough to roll out. Divide the dough into small pieces and roll out into very thin 5 inch (12cm) circles.

Filling
Melt the shortening. Add all the other ingredients except the flour and cook until the meat is browned. Stir in the flour.

Place a spoonful of mixture on a pastry circle, seal the edges with a fork and deep-fry in hot oil until golden. Drain on paper towels.

Makes 18

DON'T MISS

- Short-order plate lunches and homemade meringue pies, served at Lea's Pies in Lecompte (south of Alexandria).
- Roast beef poboys at Ray's PeGe in Monroe.
- Fried catfish just about anywhere.
- Spicy fried meat pies at Laysonne's Meat Pie Kitchen in Natchitoches.
- Ruston peaches in summertime.
- Strawberry pies at Strawn's Eat Shop in Shreveport.

The food of Northern Louisiana hasn't had the diverse influences of New Orleans or Acadiana and tends to be simple country fare with pronounced Soul Food undertones. Locals have commented that there isn't a lot of good food outside the home, but the small town diners of the region can be hidden treasures. In the larger cities of Shreveport and Monroe, Italian families have founded successful restaurant dynasties.

Many of these diners will conform to the traditional 'meat and three' configuration, meaning one serving of meat (usually a long-cooked dish like pork roast, smothered steak, or the ever-present pan-fried catfish) and a choice of three vegetables on the side. Such a meal is often accompanied by cornbread or yeast rolls, and iced tea. With the choice of dessert, usually a seasonal fruit cobbler or pie, it's a lot of food for the money, and enough to inspire an afternoon nap.

There's also a small pocket of French culture in Natchitoches and the surrounding Cane River country. The French colonialists built a fort in Natchitoches to compete with Spanish forces in neighboring Texas, and an important French trading post soon developed. However, when the Red River jumped her banks and moved 10 miles away, this little town was left stranded. The French influence in Natchitoches is still evident, and tourists come to see the architecture of this beautifully preserved little town which, as any local will tell you, was the setting for the film and play *Steel Magnolias*. Natchitoches has its own culinary specialty, the Natchitoches meat pie (fried pie stuffed with spiced beef and pork; see the recipe).

where to
eat & drink

While most trips are measured in days, a trip to New Orleans is best measured in meals. With so many restaurants and so many culinary styles, a trip to the Crescent City can be blissfully overwhelming for the hungry, curious traveler. The truly dedicated eater will turn their New Orleans visit into one extended feeding frenzy as they wander from epiphany to epiphany.

New Orleans is a sociable city and its people live to eat out, as dining here nourishes the soul and sustains the body in a single sitting. From the simple lunch counters to the white linen Creole institutions of the French Quarter, the high-spirited restaurant scene forms the cornerstone of social life for the locals. Dining out cements family as well as casual and business relationships, and few occasions pass without a celebratory meal at a favorite restaurant. And when New Orleanians aren't eating out, they are talking, thinking and arguing about it.

In practical terms, restaurant life is integral to the way that local people view their city. Well-known culinary institutions are usually included as landmarks in driving directions – "Oh, I live Uptown, between Plum Street Snowballs and the Adams Street Grocery." Ask any taxi driver for dining recommendations, and you're likely to get a litany of options, tailored to a joint's specific specialties or the driver's personal life events – "Aaaooow. My wife Bawbra an' me go to Liuzza's on Wednesdays for their eggplant and Jack Dempsey's when we want fried fish. Unless my brother-in-law Deano's with us. He always ends up draggin' us to Mandina's for the shrimp poboy and turtle soup."

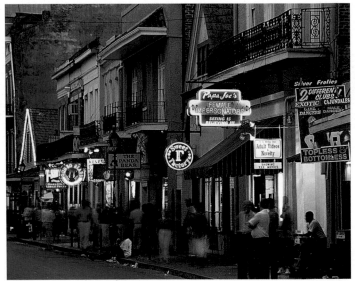

Bourbon Street at night, French Quarter

WHERE TO EAT & DRINK

Even when they're in the middle of a wonderful meal, the people of New Orleans will analyze, compare and discuss the current state of the city's active restaurant scene. The locals follow the comings and goings of sous chefs, pastry artists, and line cooks with an enthusiasm usually reserved for professional sports teams. When a new joint opens up, the average citizen knows the experience, pedigree and job history of the major kitchen players.

Supported and guided by such a demanding local market, restaurateurs are constantly trying to keep quality high and prices reasonable. Locals will splurge for dressy special occasions, but they usually frequent tried-and-true neighborhood institutions that provide good value for dollar.

Visitors naturally gravitate towards the French Quarter, which has the greatest range of eateries in the city. However, standards can vary somewhat due to the less demanding and more transient tourist trade. A restaurant that earns a local reputation for either mediocre food or questionable value will be shunned by the locals, while still packing in visitors from Minneapolis or Melbourne.

French Quarter 'tourist traps' tend to share the following traits: use of superlative descriptions like Serving the Best Gumbo/Poboys/Cajun food/Pralines in The Quarter/New Orleans/Louisiana/The World; decor that leans heavily on Mardi Gras images; and *lots* of neon. If you decide on a restaurant that exhibits one or more of these symptoms, adjust your expectations accordingly.

There is a glorious abundance of top-quality restaurants in New Orleans, suitable for every budget and taste. But in such a dynamic environment, restaurants rise, fall and fail at a rapid pace. So when you arrive, ask your taxi driver, concierge or guide for their favorites, because informed and well-fed locals are always willing to steer visitors through the latest developments. (See also New Orleans & Surrounds in the Regional Variations chapter.)

WHERE TO EAT & DRINK

THE BILL

When you eat out in Louisiana, a local sales tax is automatically added to your bill (usually 8-10% of the food cost). At sit-down establishments, you are also expected to tip waiting staff a minimum of 15%. Wages for service staff throughout the US are paltry and the customer is expected to supplement it. So, all up, you can expect to add at least 24% to the prices on the menu.

Types of Eateries
Old-Line Creole
This fine-dining subcategory represents the fancy food that made New Orleans famous. Expect a formal, historical atmosphere (especially by US standards) and menus filled with butter-rich sauces, continental French influences, and local seafood. Many of these landmarks pride themselves on preserving the New Orleans Creole tradition. The watchwords here are tradition and consistency.

Service and decorum at these local institutions is definitively old school – it's not uncommon for the waitstaff at these places to be 30-year veterans. Diners will be expected to adhere to a semi-formal dress code – jackets for gentlemen – designed to weed out the tank-top-and-shorts tourist crowd. If you can afford the relatively steep price tag, with main courses between US$20-35, a meal at one of the old-line Creole institutions is a wonderful 'old New Orleans' experience. The budget conscious can dress up for a lunchtime excursion, which is significantly less expensive than dinner seatings. Reservations are usually required.

Contemporary Cuisine
Recent trends in American cuisine have resulted in a cross-pollination of culinary styles and techniques. The global flavors of fusion cuisine and the essentialist simplicity of new American cuisine have led to exciting high-end interpretations of classic dishes that aren't bound by the rules of tradition. New Orleans' chefs, always eager to experiment with unfamiliar flavors, have come up with cuisines that they call Contemporary Creole, Nouveau Cajun, Louisiana Fusion, or New New Orleans food. Dishes from these kitchens can include crunchy fried rabbit with tasso cream sauce or panéed Gulf trout with vermouth crème fraiche and poached oysters.

Unlike old-line restaurants, where anonymous chefs uphold the house tradition, contemporary restaurants rely on high-profile chefs known for their culinary style and imagination. You can expect upscale prices, service, and wine selections at these fine dining establishments, but the atmosphere will tend toward the more stylish, as will the crowds. To get into the hottest new restaurants, book ahead as far in advance as possible.

Neighborhood Joints
For unfussy and reasonably priced regional dishes, go where the locals go, the few-frills neighborhood restaurant. The pick of this bracket all share similar characteristics: they've been around for generations; they've been staffed by the same waiters and cooks for decades; and the clientele will vary from construction workers in overalls to white-collar types.

NEW ORLEANS NOTABLES

In a town with so many exceptional restaurants, making specific recommendations should be a pretty easy task. But with countless restaurants in each category and not near enough print space to describe each establishment's notable dishes, making recommendations can be a daunting task. If you had months to explore the culinary diversity of New Orleans, you would only scratch the surface ofthe local restaurant scene. You would also weigh about 500 pounds.

Take these loose recommendations or gather your own (preferably from zealous locals or non-concierge types) and let your taste buds (and pocketbook) be your guides.

Old Line

Antoine's (713 Saint Louis St, 504.581-4422) Billed as the 'oldest restaurant in North America', Antoine's was founded in 1840 and continues its tradition of upscale Creole dishes in a formal atmosphere.

Arnaud's (813 Bienville St, 504.523-5433) The birthplace of Oysters Bienville and a fine place to try other old-school Creole dishes. Jackets for gentlemen required in the main room, but the less formal bistro-style Richileu Room caters to a more casually dressed tourist crowd.

Commander's Palace (1403 Washington Ave at Coliseum St, 504.899-8221) The flagship of the Brennan family dynasty, this Garden District favorite has been home to many of the Crescent City's most famous chefs – Paul Prudhomme and Emeril Lagasse did stints running the kitchen at Commander's Palace. Current executive chef Jamie Shannon does an admirable job continuing the establishment's tradition. Other notable restaurants in the Brennan's empire include: **Palace Café** for great bistro atmosphere on Canal Street; the venerable **Brennan's** for fantastic (if pricey) brunches; and the original **Bananas Foster** (see Bananas Foster in the Staples & Specialties chapter).

Dooky Chase's (2301 Orleans Ave, 504.821-0060) This well-regarded Creole institution is significant both for its history and haute yet homey cuisine. Owned by the charismatic chef Leah Chase, Dooky Chase's is a cornerstone of New Orleans' African American 'black Creole' community.

Galatoire's (209 Bourbon St, 504.525-2021) Great Creole food and one of New Orleans' classic lunchtime experiences. Like the other members of this category, you may have to dress up a bit, but Galatoire's food and attentive service makes it more than worth the extra trouble, even in the heat of summer.

Contemporary Cuisine

Brigtsen's (723 Dante at River Rd, 504.861-7610) This Victorian building in the Riverbend District houses the creative kitchen of Frank Brigtsen (see the boxed text Compliments to the Chefs later in this chapter). Stop in for contemporary Creole cuisine served in roadhouse portions.

NOLA (534 St Louis St, 504.522-6652) Emeril's second restaurant was designed to be local-friendly and presents his eclectic dishes in a semi-formal (but still comfortable) atmosphere (see the boxed text Compliments to the Chefs later in this chapter).

Jacques-Imo's (8324 Oak St, 504.861-0886) This tiny Uptown kitchen serves Creole classics as well as inventive variations to standing-room-only crowds nightly. Reservations required, and expect a wait at the nearby Maple Leaf Bar (see the boxed text Compliments to the Chefs).

Neighborhood Joints

Mandina's (3800 Canal St at Cortez, 504.482-0146) This Mid-City stalwart is famous for its straightforward versions of Creole and Italian dishes. Try the wonderful turtle soup spiked with sherry or delicate pan-fried soft-shell crabs.

Dunbar's Creole Cuisine (4927 Freret at Robert, 504.899-0734) Hungry travelers, rejoice. Perfectly prepared fried chicken and red beans are the deal of the century: all you can eat for under $5.

Irene's Cuisine (539 St Phillip St, 504.529-8811) This well-hidden Creole and Italian restaurant doesn't see much tourist trade, catering instead to regulars looking for specialties like garlic-heavy herbed chicken rose-marino and a decadent double-cream bread pudding.

Uglesich's (1238 Baronne St, 504.523-8571) Probably New Orleans' least kept lunchtime secret. Uglesich's is gaining a worldwide reputation, for creative seafood dishes despite being located in a thoroughly seedy neighborhood downtown. Cash only (see the boxed text Shuck Talk at Uglesich's later in this chapter).

Liuzza's (3636 Bienville at Telemachus, 504.482-9120) A dependable Mid-City Italian joint, Liuzza's specializes in tomato-based red gravy pasta dishes, french-fried onion rings, and cold beer in frosty bowling-ball-sized schooners.

Elizabeth's (601 Gallier St, 504.944-9272) This increasingly popular break-fast/lunch joint is known for gargantuan portions at disproportionately reasonable prices. You'll wait for a table at Elizabeth's, but the food makes it more than worth it.

Camellia Grill (626 S Carrollton Ave, 504.866-9573) The quintessential lunch counter is located near the end of the St Charles streetcar line. Egg dishes, burgers, and other simple diner fare are what Camellia is known for, along with service that borders on theatre.

Camellia Grill, New Orleans

French Quarter Standards
Central Grocery (923 Decatur St, 504.523-1620) This well-stocked import grocery and delicatessen is reputedly the home of the muffuletta. Grab your order to go or belly up to one of the tables at the back of the store. Pack your luggage with a few jars of garlicky olive salad.

Mother's (401 Poydras St, 504.523-9656) Within easy striking distance of both the French Quarter and the CBD, the thoroughly 'discovered' Mother's is a regular stop for tourist groups, and is usually crowded as a result. Great poboys and breakfast specials dominate the menu, along with Creole and Soul Food standards.

Oyster Bars
Acme Oyster House (724 Iberville St, 504.522-5973) Tourists and locals constantly pack this French Quarter oyster bar, making 'The Acme' a good eavesdropping and people-watching spot. Grab a dozen, slurp a beer and keep your eyes and ears open.

Casamento's (4330 Magazine St, 504.895-9761) On the border of the Garden District, Casamento's is a neighborhood standout with its amazing fully tiled interior. The specialty here is tasty lard-fried oysters. Summer visitors beware – Casamento's shuts down between June and September and every Monday.

The decor at a neighborhood joint may lack the polish of a high-end restaurant, but these places are less concerned with appearances than with high-quality food and unpretentious service. They tend to be comfortable, warming and welcoming, and whether you're dining solo or with a group, you'll feel at ease.

These establishments are usually extremely busy during the lunch rush (12-2pm) as well as during standard evening dinner hours (7-9pm). They rarely take reservations (exceptions are sometimes made for large groups) and often function on a 'cash or local check only' basis. Typically there will be a small wine list, as well as a bar offering a wide choice of beers and mixed drinks.

Oyster Bars

Even if you're a bit squeamish about eating live seafood, no trip to New Orleans is complete without a 'dozen raw and a beer' at a local oyster bar.

Hard-working shuckers work like banter-friendly sushi chefs as they rip through piles of rocky shells with gloved hands and blunt, thick-bladed oyster knives.

Hardcore oyster bars can be a little intimidating for the newcomer, like you've just stepped into the ceremonies of an arcane culinary cult. Regular patrons each have their own oyster ritual, which takes on meditative qualities. It's fun to watch the different routines – slurp, pause, and stare into space is the most common. The salty gulps are usually punctuated with sips of cold beer.

While many oyster aficionados gasp at the very notion of adding any other substance to their beloved bivalve, it is not unusual to see non-purists dipping the raw oyster into a self-seasoned tomato-based cocktail sauce, plopping the oyster on a crispy saltine cracker and chewing the lot (see Cocktail Sauce in the Staples & Specialties chapter). Oyster bars usually have a selection of sauces within reach for your personal slurping and seasoning pleasure.

Diners

Specializing in short-order cooking and long-simmering plate lunches, diners provide an inexpensive opportunity to sample traditional fare with service that's quick enough to keep pace with modern life. In New Orleans and other cities of the region, diners may be open around the clock to accommodate insomniacs and post-nightclub hunger pangs. Food ranges from burgers, sandwiches, pies and waffles to more regional dishes such gumbo, jambalaya, étouffée, red beans and rice, fried seafood and the ever-present poboy.

The Acme Oyster House on Iberville Street in the French Quarter, New Orleans

WHERE TO EAT & DRINK

SHUCK TALK AT UGLESICH'S

We showed up at Uglesich's well ahead of the lunch rush – Chris figured that an 11am arrival would just about guarantee us a table. The dining room at the famed local dive only holds about 30 people at a time, so it's better to be safe than sorry. But even an hour before midday, the parking lot and dining room were both packed.

On this particular January morning, the tiny joint was wall-to-wall with starched shirts and silk ties – it was like we'd discovered a nest of lawyers at feeding time. After looking over the menu, Chris turned to 'Mr Tony' (owner Anthony Uglesich) and asked about the crowd. "They're from the Federal prosecutor's convention downtown – and they wanted to eat early." He shrugged and scribbled down our orders. "Here's your number. You can wait at the bar."

The broad-shouldered man behind the bar pulled out his thick-blade knife, looked up from his work, and asked us a simple question. "How many y'all need today?"

A New Orleans classic, Uglesich's is an almost microscopic restaurant located in a questionable industrial neighborhood near downtown. It's been in business since 1924 and is one of the restaurants where the New Orleans' star chefs eat on *their* days off. The fried seafood consistently rates among the best in town, no mean feat in this land of fishophiles. Anthony Uglesich is the creative mind behind the kitchen and the man behind the cash register, but during the lunch rush wait, you usually end up talking to the guys behind the oyster bar.

While the cooks are cranking out orders of tasty crawfish fettuccine, poboys to fight over, fantastic fries, and downright spiritual fish dishes, the guys behind the tiny oyster bar shuck the rocky mollusks for both the waiting customers and the kitchen. And all the while, they keep the patter going.

"Them oysters look pretty good!" Chris yelled over the din of the lawyers. This time of year, when the Gulf waters are cold, the oysters are at their best – fat, plump and flavorful.

"Yeah, they're good all right." The guy on the other side of the bar flicked his blunt-bladed knife and in two clean strokes split open a rough oyster and cut the bivalve's tough muscle from the shell. With a fluid overhand motion, he laid the newly shucked oyster (now on the proverbial half shell) on a tray, grabbed another rocky shellfish and started over. He made the whole thing look as easy as breathing. Within seconds

*One of the past great 'shuckers',
Uglesich's Restaurant, New Orleans*

a full dozen of the plump morsels were ready for a squeeze of lemon. He pushed us the tray and dug into the next dozen.

"But *man* ..." he stopped for a second, and shook his head. "You shoulda tasted 'em last week." Conditions were at their seasonal peak, and the local fishermen had brought in a legendary haul. Even though he shucks hundreds of these little beauties each day, we could tell that the week before, our oyster man had seen a sack of perfect oysters. For a second the whole place, lawyers and all, dropped in volume and breathed between bites.

The oyster man took another breath, grinned, and the glint of his eye ricocheted off his knife. "Man, when they're that good ..." he shook his head one more time, "they just *go*."

Then, quick as a flash, three more cuts, five more oysters, and the next salty dozen was ready to go. Not a bad way to spend a 20-minute wait.

Pableaux Johnson

Country Restaurants & Lunch Counters

Found outside the metropolis, these establishments can resemble an urban neighborhood joint or a bustling short-order diner. These small, often family-run establishments are the natural habitat of the traditional 'pie and coffee' afternoon snack, as well as the plate lunch (see the boxed text The Plate Lunch later in this chapter). In Southern Louisiana, you are most likely to encounter Cajun specialties like red beans, jambalaya and chicken fricassee, while the diners of Northern Louisiana will likely serve more Soul Food offerings like black-eyed peas, chicken and dumplings, or smothered pork chops.

Country restaurants can range from small affairs with half a dozen tables to large barn-like structures where hundreds of families can be accommodated for Sunday lunch. Some places serve lunch only and close at 2pm on the dot. Others stay open until 7pm, perhaps a little later on Friday evenings. Most places only accept cash or personal checks, and it's pretty unlikely that they will take advance bookings.

Poboy Shops and Other Fast Food

If you're constrained by time, budget, or just want a quick snack, New Orleans has quick, inexpensive midday fare at its countless poboy shops, neighborhood groceries, and even gas stations. A common gas station snack in Acadiana is hot boudin served by the link and a soda or beer to wash it down (see Boudin in the Staples & Specialties chapter). In the realm of plastic franchise restaurants, a local chain called Popeye's specializes in spicy fried chicken and serves fast-food versions of regional dishes such as shrimp étouffée and jambalaya.

A poboy shop in the French Quarter, New Orleans

BOILING POINTS

Take the pygmy cousin of the Atlantic lobster, plunge it into boiling water blood-red with cayenne pepper, then spill the whole mess onto a paper-covered table. Pick up a steaming red crawfish off the pile, tear off its cephalothorax and strip sections of protective shell from its tail. Bite off the meat, inhale through the dismembered head cavity, and throw the shells on an ever-growing mountain of empties. Repeat as needed.

This simple ritual – eating boiled crawfish – is at the heart of Cajun food culture, and at its best in informal restaurants called boiling points. Though you'll be able to find boiled crawfish in New Orleans, these road-side joints that dot Southern Louisiana roads are the best place to sample boiled crawfish in its purest form.

As the name suggests, these often ramshackle establishments specialize in fresh boiled seafood, served simply and in great quantities. Whether indoors or out, dining rooms are informal, and often border on institutional. Patio seating will usually be on picnic tables; inside tables are covered with protective plastic tablecloths. The beer is cheap and plentiful, and the catch of the day is served by the 'order' (3-5lb or 1-2kg) on circular aluminum trays.

Boiling point menus vary by season, since they reflect whatever shellfish is currently crawling about in the local fishermen's nets. During summer, boiled crabs and shrimp are common, while in the late spring, crawfish from the wilds of the Atchafalaya Basin or local farms are the special of the day. The best time to sample boiled crawfish is from roughly mid-February to June, just as the local waters are starting to warm up after the short winter chill.

Patrons enjoying a meal of crab at D.I.'s, near Eunice

WHERE TO EAT & DRINK

Crabs being dumped in the boil at the Guiding Star, New Iberia

The Boiling Process

Boiling points cook hundreds of pounds of seafood every day and their equipment reflects this exaggerated sense of scale. Huge pots, measured in the tens of gallons and fitted with special basket inserts, are set to boil over industrial gas burners. Once heated, flavorings are added to the burbling pot. Onions, lemons, cayenne pepper and commercially mixed seafood boils are added to spice up the water (see Seafood Boil in the Staples & Specialties chapter). Once it has been sufficiently spiced, the huge batch of bubbling 'boil water' will resemble a cauldron of boiling blood.

Prior to the boil, live crawfish (maroon to black in color) are soaked in a salt-heavy water solution for up to an hour. This process, called purging, forces the squirming shellfish to expel mud and other internal goop. After a quick second rinse (plain water this time) the fitted basket is filled with crawling critters, red potatoes and cobs of sweet corn. The basket is then lowered into the boiling water. About 15 minutes later, the crawfish are lifted from the pot – bright red, steaming and ready for the table. The water is respiced, the basket refilled, and another batch of crawfish is readied for the boil.

The 'Peel & Suck'

The process of eating boiled crawfish is, in a way, as complex as the cooking process. But if you can identify the meaty part of a lobster (that's the tail, for the uninitiated) then you already know the basics of crawfish anatomy.

Your job is to twist the crawfish's tasty tail from its claw/head assembly, then to remove the tail's layer of protective shell and thin 'vein' of intestine. What remains is a small bite of pure crawfish meat, the taste of Cajun Louisiana. As you savor the crawfish's sweet, rich flavor, discard the remaining tail fin and reach for the next one.

The easiest way to learn this no-utensils-allowed peeling process is to get a quick demonstration from a local. Staff in any restaurant are accustomed to explaining the technique, so don't be afraid to ask. The key to filling up on these tiny critters is establishing a steady peeling rhythm. Speed and fluency of motion will come with practice, and by the bottom of your tray, you'll have thoroughly messy hands, burning lips, and a contented soul.

The time-honored practice of 'sucking the head' (with all its overtly sexual connotations) is a process of getting to the yellow-orange 'fat' located inside the crawfish's cephalothorax ('body' for non-biologists). The 'fat' is actually the liver of the crawfish, where spices collect during the boiling process.

One common method of 'getting the fat out' so to speak, involves treating a de-tailed crawfish like a cigar and inhaling where the tail socket connects to the body. Another, more effective method requires a hands-on approach – run your pinky finger inside of the body to harvest the tasty goo. Remove, lick and repeat with the next hapless beastie. Either way, Dr Freud would definitely approve.

Jean Bourque, breaking crabs at the Guiding Star, New Iberia, Louisiana

An Important Hand-Washing Tip

After a few bites into your crawfish epiphany, you'll notice the pronounced burn of red pepper on your hands as well as your mouth. The inherently messy peeling process invariably coats your hands and mouth with spicy crawfish juice. If you have any tiny cuts on your hands, they'll start stinging soon after you start peeling. This pain is an unavoidable and integral part of the crawfish experience.

There is, however, another more profound and personal pain that should be avoided at all costs. In many boiling points, you'll see hand-washing sinks in the dining rooms, mysterious aluminum rods and signs imploring patrons to wash their hands before using the restroom rather than after. The reason is that traces of cayenne and other spices on the hands can act as a painful irritant to 'soft tissues' (eyes and genitals). If you don't lather up your hands before unzipping, you may end up with more than a pepper-burned mouth. Rubbing your hands on the aluminum rod also has the effect of neutralizing the pepper's burning chemicals. Don't say we didn't warn you.

WHERE TO EAT & DRINK

Foreign Fare

Just as it has throughout history, New Orleans opens its arms and kitchen doors to international culinary influences from the four corners of the globe. In a city that loves to eat, new discoveries and influences are always welcome, and you'll notice that foreign influences are even creeping into many upscale restaurants. You'll also find a wide variety of ethnic restaurants in the confines of the Crescent City.

With its manifold pasta and pizza options, Italian is the most popular ethnic cuisine in town, especially the locally adapted Creolized version. The riverfront side of the French Quarter was the original home of the Sicilian community and there are still some Sicilian-run family restaurants peppered through the city's other neighborhoods.

New Orleans' Mid-City district is home to the US's highest concentration of Vietnamese immigrants and their spicy national cuisine fits in well with local tastes. The same goes for the well-established Cuban and Cuban-American community.

Outside New Orleans, there are far fewer ethnic options beyond a few Italian restaurants, lackluster Mexican establishments and Americanized Chinese offerings. In places where Cajun influences are strong, Asian menus have adapted to local demand by offering dishes like crawfish fried rice and shrimp-heavy spring rolls.

Vegetarians & Vegans

The same cooking techniques that make Louisiana food so flavorful can also make mealtime rather challenging for the vegetarian traveler. The common use of 'flavoring meats' and meat-based stocks means that many apparently flesh-free vegetable dishes may well include a bit of ham, sausage or seafood. It's not that the cooks of Louisiana are out to persecute the herbivorous diner – it's just that they come from thoroughly omnivorous traditions.

However, as the average American becomes more aware of the flesh-free aesthetic, more options are appearing on the local restaurant scene. There are a few restaurants catering exclusively to vegetarians and most upscale places will be able to assemble something, even if they don't have vegetarian dishes on the menu. Italian restaurants, with their pastas and tomato-based red gravy dishes are good bets.

With some planning, you will be able to enjoy the regional cuisine without compromise or despair. Firstly, demi-vegetarians (people who eat seafood) will have no problems as seafood is one of the region's culinary strengths, although you should double check with staff because sausage and ham can also be added, particularly in seafood gumbo.

Gumbo z'herbes, a green gumbo made with a hearty variety of turnip, collard, spinach and other greens is a meatless Lenten staple that many Creole restaurants offer year round. Just ask whether the roux was made with butter or oil and if there are any pork products used in the cooking process. Neighborhood joints shouldn't provide any difficulty as they will invariably have bean and vegetable side dishes, which you can combine to make up a substantial meal. While vegetables and beans used to be cooked in pig fat, these days most places use vegetable oil, although you should check first. A muffuletta without the Italian meats (cheeses and olive salad only) is a good way to sample a reasonable meatless facsimile of the local sandwich specialty. It will be easier to find vegetarian infrastructure in the bigger cities and towns, but don't overlook local country diners, which will have a wide selection of vegetable dishes for the choosing. Vegans should steer clear of cornbread, since it's usually prepared with a batter that includes eggs and milk.

THE PLATE LUNCH

One of the standbys of any informal Louisiana restaurant is the plate lunch that's advertised on handmade signs from Shreveport to the coast. You'll see the magic phrase at small-town diners, at gas station mini-marts, and outside small houses in residential neighborhoods. Nothing fancy, nothing special, but the words 'plate lunch' mean that there's usually a lot of good food for very reasonable prices.

Travelers who have traversed the Deep South will recognize the plate lunch as a variation on the classic Soul Food 'meat and three' mealtime configuration. A serving of slow-cooked meat (such as round steak and gravy, smothered chicken, or fried fish) is accompanied with a choice of several pre-cooked vegetables (such as okra, corn maque choux, black-eyed peas or turnip greens). The resulting plate is rounded off by cornbread, yeast rolls, or plain slices of white bread, as well as a glass of iced tea. The selection of a plate lunch will reflect the town's dominant cuisine: red beans and rice with sausage, jambalaya, and shrimp stew in Cajun Country; chicken and dumplings or roast beef in Northern Louisiana.

Many plate-lunch establishments have simple sit-down dining rooms, but others (such as those in tiny market kitchens) will serve the daily specials in styrofoam 'to go' boxes. If you're traveling through rural areas, these impromptu dining opportunities often represent good, solid local cooking at prices that rival the mostly plastic fast-food 'bargain burger' meals.

Pableaux Johnson

STREET FOOD

Though it may not have a positive reputation, the street food of New Orleans can be as interesting (if not appealing) as the city's restaurant offerings. Look for these trademark offerings as you meander around the city between meals.

Lucky Dogs

Priceless works of pop art or culinary travesties? Your verdict on these 7-foot weenie-shaped carts will be largely dependent on your level of intoxication. Most locals (and sober folk of all persuasions) tend to admire these migratory sausage-vending carts from afar, while the more 'altered' visitors flock to them for between-bar sustenance. If you fit the latter description, load up your hot dog with sauce, mustard, or any other condiment, and relish the presence of this surreal New Orleans institution. Are Lucky Dogs any good? As a nostalgic veteran once put it: "Not exactly *good*, but when you're walking down Bourbon Street, they're good *enough.*"

Snowballs for sale

Snowballs (Snow Cones)

These brightly colored and amazingly sweet concoctions are a godsend on insufferable New Orleans summer days. The recipe for a snowball couldn't be simpler – fill a paper cup with shaved ice and douse it liberally with sugar-sweet flavored syrup. During the hot months, bare bones shacks and portable trailers magically appear on the streets, as do lines of overheated kids and adults. Two of the more popular flavors are 'Popeye' (deep green spearmint) and sapphire-blue bubble gum. The cool, refreshing sweetness can cool your body and dye your tongue for hours. The Uptown gold standard for this smooth, sweet treat can be found at William's Plum Street Snowballs (1300 Burdette at Plum Street, 504.866-7996).

Roman Chewing Candy

In the middle of the CBD or near a JazzFest stage, you might see a white horse-drawn carriage peddling this old-school sweet treat. Similar to old fashioned tooth-tugging taffy, Roman Chewing Candy comes in three flavors (chocolate, strawberry and vanilla).

Playing a trumpet in the square with a Lucky Dogs hot dog stand in the background, New Orleans

COMPLIMENTS TO THE CHEFS

New Orleans is a town that both respects and reveres its cooks – from the fast-fingered poboy makers to the hard working line cooks that make the city's restaurants hum. Some of these chefs are tourist draws unto themselves, drawing food groupies from around the world. Here are a few of the celebrity chefs that represent the Crescent City.

Paul Prudhomme

The globally recognized owner/chef of K-Paul's Louisiana Kitchen, Paul Prudhomme is largely responsible for bringing traditional Cajun cooking to the world's culinary radar screen. His jolly face and spherical profile grace cookbook covers, TV shows, and his own private line of eponymous Magic Seasonings. The youngest of 13 children, this Opelousas-born chef learned his trade in his family's rural home kitchen. He came to public notice as the executive chef at Commander's Palace, where he honed his skills, creating such dishes as the often imitated Blackened Redfish. In 1986 the American Culinary Federation named Paul Prudhomme 'Culinarian of the Year' and he was the first American to receive the French Republic's *Merité Agricole*.

Susan Spicer

If Prudhomme brought New Orleans food to the world, then Susan Spicer brought her distinctive brand of world food to New Orleans. This was the result of growing up in many countries and under the wing of her mother, who was always open to culinary experimentation. The food at Susan Spicer's reward-winning restaurant, Bayona, features flavors of the Mediterranean, Alsace, Asia, India and the Southwest. Her latest venture, Spice, Inc. combines a market, cafe and cookery school.

Emeril Lagasse

Robust, energetic and a tireless master of self-promotion, Emeril Lagasse is the current high-profile star of New Orleans cooking. Born in the Portuguese community of Fall River, Massachusetts, Emeril Lagasse started his culinary career working at a local bakery before a storied career that landed him in New Orleans. Like his predecessor Prudhomme, Emeril came to prominence as an innovative executive chef at Commander's Palace before opening his first restaurant, Emeril's in the city's warehouse district. The success that followed led to the French Quarter's more informal NOLA and Lagasse's resurrection of a local institution – The Delimonico Restaurant and Bar. His signature New New Orleans cuisine is featured at outposts in glitzy Las Vegas and Orlando, Florida. His animated antics and showmanship have made his cooking shows on cable TV's Food Network nationwide hits and built 'The BÁM Man' a following among kitchenphobes and foodies alike.

Frank Brigtsen
An early alumnus of K-Paul's kitchen, Frank Brigtsen now runs an intimate self-titled restaurant in the Riverbend district, where he showcases his contemporary and sophisticated takes on Creole dishes. Brigtsen is known for balancing bold flavors and delicate textures, especially with local game selections such as duck and rabbit.

Jack Leonardi and Austin Leslie
The culinary team behind Jacques-Imo's, Leonardi and Leslie bring two distinctly different backgrounds to this wildly popular neighborhood restaurant. Leslie, former chef of the legendary (and sadly defunct) Creole-joint Chez Helene, joined Leonardi, a veteran of the local nightclub scene and K-Paul's, to open the insanely popular Uptown establishment. The results are astounding dishes that mix modern creativity (seafood-stuffed acorn squash in saffron broth) with rock-solid Creole classics like fried chicken and stuffed bell peppers.

Anne Kearney
Anne Kearney has learned her trade from the best sources since moving to New Orleans from her native Ohio. She has worked with Emeril Lagasse, as well as with the late John Neal – the founder of Peristyle, where she is now the chef and owner. Although Kearney is now a well-known chef, her restaurant remains an intimate establishment, serving what she calls 'bistro fare'. Her culinary style has Provençal origins, yet is forever changing as she gleans styles and tastes from other sources.

Anne Kearney

Children

Apart from the city's upscale establishments, the majority of eateries are fairly friendly towards family dining. Restaurants will usually have a children's menu offering simple foods such as fried catfish nuggets, chicken strips, fried shrimp, spaghetti and meatballs, and peanut butter and jelly sandwiches. If your child is set on a dish from the main menu, ask about the spice level before ordering. Often they can either ratchet down the spice or suggest an appropriately tame alternative.

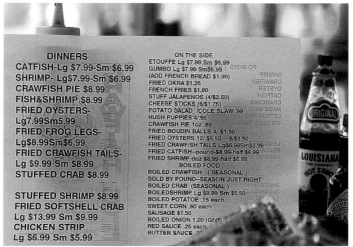

A menu at the Best Tails In Town, Natchitoches

Understanding the Menu

If you're not from the US, the important difference is that the typical restaurant meal is divided into three sections: the appetizer (starting course), entree (main course) and dessert. Most restaurants will present a printed menu and have the daily specials recited by the waitstaff. At country restaurants serving plate lunches the menu might be completely verbal, so pay attention if you don't see a blackboard or printed menus.

You may also encounter specialized restaurants that only serve one item cooked in one way only, for example fried catfish or boiled crawfish. In this case, all you have to do is say how much you want as the food will be sold by the plate, pound or piece.

Camellia Grill, New Orleans

WHERE TO EAT & DRINK

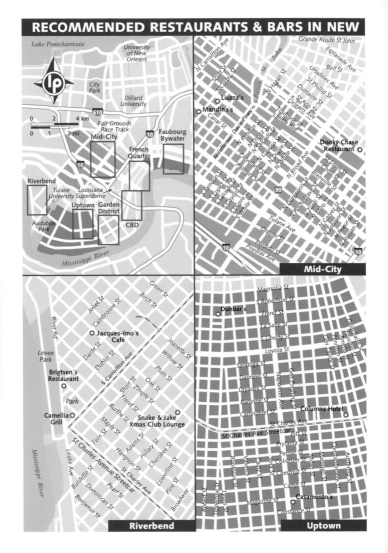

RECOMMENDED RESTAURANTS & BARS IN NEW

Mid-City

Riverbend

Uptown

Lake Pontchartrain

University of New Orleans

City Park

Dillard University

Fair Grounds Race Track

Mid-City

Faubourg Bywater

French Quarter

Riverbend

Tulane University

Louisiana Superdome

Uptown

Garden District

CBD

Audubon Park

Mississippi River

Grande Route St John

Esplanade Ave

Liuzza's

Mandina's

Dooky Chase Restaurant

Tulane Ave

Gravier St

Perdido Ave

Poydras Ave

Green St

Birch St

Joliet St

Cambronne St

Jacques-Imo's Café

Jeanette St

Willow St

Dante St

Dublin St

Oak St

Plum St

Short St

Zimple St

Treret St

Brigtsen's Restaurant

Burthe St

Camellia Grill

Snake & Jake Xmas Club Lounge

Maple St

Fern St

Adams St

Hillary St

Cherokee St

St Charles Avenue Streetcar

Hampson St

Lowerline St

Pine St

Burdette St

Dominican St

Pearl St

Broadway

Benjamin St

Leake Ave

Mississippi River

Magnolia St

S Roberson St

Freret St

La Salle St

S Liberty St

Loyola St

Dunbar's

Saratoga St

Danneel St

Dryades St

Baronne St

Carondelet St

Columns Hotel

St Charles Ave

St Charles Ave Streetcar

Prytania St

Perrier St

Coliseum St

Chestnut St

Camp St

Magazine St

Casamento's

Constance St

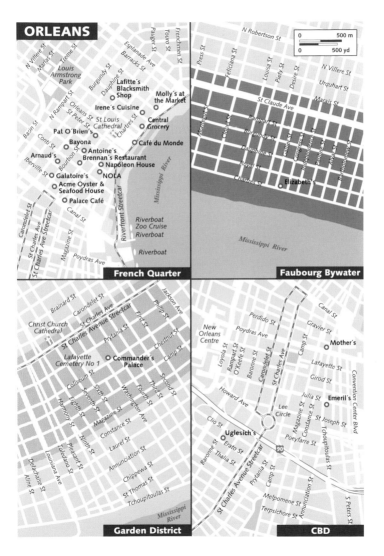

ORLEANS

French Quarter

N Villere St
Marais St
Treme St
Esplanade Ave
Pauger St
Touro St
Frenchmen St
Barracks St
Louis Armstrong Park
Burgundy St
Dauphine St
N Rampart St
Bourbon St
St Peter St
Orleans Ave
St Louis Cathedral
St Charles St
Conti St
Bienville St
Iberville St
Bourbon St
Basin St

Lafitte's Blacksmith Shop
Irene's Cuisine
Molly's at the Market
Pat O'Brien's
Bayona
Central Grocery
Arnaud's
Antoine's
Café du Monde
Brennan's Restaurant
Napoleon House
Galatoire's
NOLA
Acme Oyster & Seafood House
Palace Café

Carondelet St
St Charles Ave Streetcar
St Charles Ave
Canal St
Magazine St
Poydras Ave

Mississippi River
Riverfront Streetcar
Riverboat
Zoo Cruise
Riverboat
Riverboat

Faubourg Bywater

N Robertson St
Press St
Feliciana St
Louisa St
Piety St
Desire St
N Villere St
Urquhart St
Marais St
St Claude Ave
Montegut St
Clouet St
Rampart St
Burgundy St
Dauphine St
Royal St
Charles St
Gallier St
France St
Independence St
Mandeville St
Spain St

Elizabeth's

Mississippi River

0   500 m
0   500 yd

Garden District

Brainard St
Carondelet St
St Charles Ave
Jackson Ave
Philip St
First St
Christ Church Cathedral
St Charles Avenue Streetcar
Prytania St
Chestnut St
Camp St
Lafayette Cemetery No 1
Commander's Palace
Coliseum St
Sixth St
Seventh St
Second St
Third St
Washington Ave
Fourth St
Harmony St
Magazine St
Constance St
Eighth St
Ninth St
Laurel St
Pleasant St
Toledano St
Louisiana Ave
Annunciation St
Delachaise St
Aline St
Chippewa St
St Thomas St
Tchoupitoulas St

Mississippi River

CBD

Canal St
Perdido St
Gravier St
Poydras Ave
New Orleans Centre
Loyola Ave
Rampart St
O'Keefe St
Baronne St
Carondelet St
St Charles Ave
Camp St
Mother's
Lafayette St
Girod St
Convention Center Blvd
Howard Ave
Julia St
Emeril's
Clio St
Lee Circle
Magazine St
Constance St
St Joseph St
Uglesich's
Erato St
Baronne St
Thalia St
Poeyfarre St
Tchoupitoulas St
90
St Charles Avenue Streetcar
Prytania St
Camp St
Melpomene St
Annunciation St
Terpsichore St
S Peters St

WHERE TO EAT & DRINK

Where to Drink

New Orleans has more bars per capita than any other city in the US and, whatever your inclination, you'll find one to suit. If your pleasure includes piano bar singalongs, late-night techno dancing, or old-fashioned falling-down drunkenness then get yourself down to the city's most famous drag, Bourbon Street. Most tourists end up here, hell-bent on writing themselves off for the day, weekend, or carnival season. But few of the natives stomp this ground so if it's local color you're after, seek out the bars in other streets of the Quarter and beyond (see the Recommended Restaurants & Bars in New Orleans map earlier in this chapter).

Many bars serve mixed drinks or specialty cocktails with colorful and menacing names like Hurricane or Hand Grenade. Most bars will have a happy hour early in the evening, during which they offer indecently cheap booze. Publications including *The Gambit* (free weekly newspaper) and *Offbeat* (monthly music magazine) have information on these happy hours as well as entertainment listings. Alternatively, the barkers outside the bars will let you know what's on special. Drinks are moderately priced and you should leave a small tip for the bar person (averaging from pocket change to $1 per drink).

Once you are out of New Orleans, local barrooms tend to be of the windowless variety. You can't see what is going on – and it is probably nothing more than a few local guys having a few beers and shooting pool – but you are going to have to go in to find out.

Bourbon Street ramblers at night, New Orleans

THE OLDEST BAR IN AMERICA?

Lafitte's Blacksmith Shop, Bourbon Street

If you keep walking up Bourbon Street, out of the raucous carnival gaiety and towards the more sedate residential section, you'll come across Lafitte's Blacksmith Shop, a shop so improbably rustic that you'll think you've stumbled onto a movie set. This is in fact a bar, and not just any old bar.

Step into the dark interior, buy a drink and take a street-side seat so you can listen to the commentary of the many tour guides leading their party by. One guide will point in your direction and proclaim this to be "the oldest bar in America." Another will say "the oldest building housing a bar in America." Local historians are still slugging that one out.

In truth, the building is the second oldest in New Orleans (the oldest is the Ursaline Convent) and it was built in 1722. It survived the two devastating fires that swept through New Orleans in the 1700s and there has been a bar in the building since the mid 1800s.

The name Lafitte refers to the shady local hero Jean Lafitte, often glamorously referred to as a pirate but who was actually a profiteer who made his money in slave-trading and other dodgy dealings. Along with his brother, Pierre, Jean Lafitte set up a blacksmith's shop in this building as a cover for covert operations. The French turned a blind eye to his dealings, but things changed when the Americans took over the colony. The newly appointed Governor was about to arrest Lafitte when the Battle of New Orleans broke out. Lafitte rounded up a huge band of local men who joined the local military in whipping the pants off the British. Lafitte became a local hero although rumor has it that he actually sat the battle out on a boat moored just off the coast.

Legend states that part of Lafitte's ill-gotten gains are hidden under the chimney that sits in the center of the bar. He is reputed to have killed a man and buried him here so the ghost would protect his booty. Come back at night when the bar is candlelit and you just might see the ghoulish guardian, if you drink enough that is.

Charmaine O'Brien

NIGHTCAP AT THE SNAKE & JAKE

Just before bedtime, and I'm sipping on a good stiff bourbon in a bar that feels like the womb. A couple of newly-tattooed Tulane students relax with legs entwined on an aging naugahyde love seat. Groups of off-duty bartenders are unwinding from busy shifts at tourist bars in the Quarter. In an hour or so, working musicians will drag in for one last drink before sunrise. Dreadlocked regulars sip in stonefaced silence. A percussive CD of local R&B ("It's last year's Bo Dollis," the bartender nods from the keg, "Kicks ass, hunh?") provides a smooth, energetic soundtrack in a barroom with seven-foot ceilings. It's three o'clock in the morning and things are just getting started at the Snake & Jake.

Secreted away on a small residential street, the venerable Snake & Jake Xmas Club Lounge is the best known unadvertised dive in New Orleans. The building itself is little more than a flimsy sheet-metal shack containing a few 1960s couches, some institutional metal chairs, and a makeshift bar. With no visble sign on the outside, The Jake (as it is known by Uptown regulars) is a part of the neighborhood landscape, and an in-crowd draw for increasing numbers of visiting hipsters. Luckily, it's around the corner from my usual New Orleans crash pad – convenient for a nice nightcap.

The brew selection is surprisingly broad for a neighborhood beer joint – local Abita on tap, along with Guinness and a few other well-respected ales. The dimly-lit bar mirror shows reflections of single-malt scotches, aging rye whiskies and quick-draw shot tequilas – a comforting range of liquors from super-premium to decidedly lowbrow.

In other cities, this ramshackle labor of love wouldn't even exist. Zoning regulations would restrict drinking establishments in designated commercial zones. Stringent health codes would keep a big man named Goat from firing up the barbecue grill out front on Saints' game Sundays. But here in the working-class section of New Orleans, not far from gothic universities and showcase homes of St Charles Avenue, the Snake & Jake putters along in all its subdued, late-night glory.

A few songs later, and my whisky's almost gone. One quick swig and a wave to the bartender later, I'm on my way out the creaky front door, passing an inbound after-gig gaggle of musicians. They're right on time, and I'm only steps from home. You gotta love this town.

Pableaux Johnson

shopping

& markets

As it is in the rest of the country, shopping in New Orleans and the rural sections of Louisiana has a distinctly modern feel to it. But although the homogenizing effect of the modern supermarket has touched this region, there's still a pronounced sense of the unique and local on the shelves of Louisiana's mega-marts. And for the canny shopper, there are distinct opportunities for carrying away the authentic tastes of the region's cuisine.

History

Fifty years ago the people of Louisiana did a good deal of their food shopping in small local groceries and specialty shops. Local dairies, butchers, bakeries and fishmongers served their communities with fresh produce. This was a pre-refrigeration era, and people shopped daily in these local markets and stores, which also doubled as community meeting places.

Outside the Central Grocery, New Orleans

In the more rural areas, diverse family gardens were important sources of fresh, seasonal produce, especially for folks living far removed from even small country stores.

But with the advent of cheap shipping methods and factory farming, the nature of American food changed significantly. Fruit and vegetable varieties were chosen for durability rather than for flavor – the better to survive 1500-mile journeys from field to final consumer. The same went for the custom-bred livestock and poultry that provide today's leaner meats and less flavorful boneless chicken pieces. Processed, prepackaged foods also took the place of previously home-cooked meals.

What were once seasonal crops, such as freshly picked tangy tomatoes or crisp winter apples, have now become affordable perennial necessities. But anyone who has bit into a garden-fresh Creole tomato can attest to the cost of modernity. The imported hothouse tomatoes available through the winter months have a mealy texture and none of the juicy flavor of the vine-ripened variety. Workaday tomatoes are now picked green for ease of shipping and are ripened with methane gas. During the American warm season, apples are shipped in from as far as New Zealand by ocean-going steamer.

SHOPPING

Enter the Supermarket

In most of modern America, the all-in-one supermarket (in some form or other) has replaced the separate specialty shops that made up the edible commerce of earlier years. In just about every town and city you'll recognize a variant of the huge and homogenized national chain stores – very cost efficient, round-the-clock convenient, and utterly soulless.

Still, these leviathans account for the vast majority of America's food buying, even in independent regions like Louisiana. The independent baker, delicatessen, pharmacy, newsagency, hardware store, fresh produce purveyor or butcher are starting to become an endangered species as supermarkets perform all these functions under one convenient roof. It appears that many people are willing to forgo local quality and personal attention for the opportunity to park their car and enter an air-conditioned wonderland of excess packaging, television-advertised brands, 74 choices of any product and piped muzak. If you like supermarket shopping or regard supermarkets as fascinating sites for a bit of culinary anthropology, then make sure you visit one in the region.

Ironically, there has been a recent return to the qualities of the older days, in the form of modern day boutique markets and natural food stores. Boutique markets are likely to put gourmet trappings on quality seasonal produce or locally produced meats in exchange for premium-level prices. Natural food stores are more likely to put a premium on products raised without chemical pesticides (organic) or processed with fewer additives than standard supermarket brands. Either way, straying from the dreaded supermarket will hit your wallet.

Luckily for the local food culture, there are still authentic vestiges of food shopping to be found both in the small towns of Louisiana and the neighborhoods of New Orleans proper.

Inside the Central Grocery, New Orleans

Places to Shop
Seafood Markets

Because of the major role seafood plays in the local diet, many consumers are less likely to trust a supermarket with something as delicate as fresh fish or shrimp. And since commercial establishments focus so much on cost efficiency, there's a tendency for their seafood to be frozen for shipping and thawed in the grocery's display cases. Good for the shippers, but terrible for the fish.

Fishmongers at King Rogers Seafood Market & Deli, New Orleans

Instead of compromising taste for the sake of convenience, many people in Louisiana patronize the many local free-standing seafood markets that are scattered about the residential districts of New Orleans and the smaller towns of the state. Seafood markets are especially important in Acadiana, where freshly caught fish (and locally caught crawfish) are matters of near-spiritual importance. You can expect these small markets to have the pick of the local nets, and imports from other waters only if absolutely necessary.

Truck Stands

This automotive vestige of the old farmer's market can be found alongside the many smaller roads throughout the state. A farmer or other enterprising soul will pack a truck with their produce, park next to a busy road and advertise their wares on crude handwritten signs. In summer, truck stands will sell the best blood-red Creole tomatoes or whole watermelons. It's the next best thing to picking them yourself, and often the pick of the local seasonal crop. In Northern Louisiana, truck stands are likely to sell sweet corn, crunchy pecans, or Ruston peaches when they're at the peak of ripeness. Acadiana natives are accustomed to seeing these improvised roadside stands selling shrimp or live blue crabs by the pound. Some larger stands have a more permanent feel to them, and often supplement their fresh offerings with local honey, jams and pickles and home-packaged treats like Aunt Jane's Eggplant Relish.

Roadside signs

Meat Markets

The smaller towns of Cajun Country are home to meat markets of regional renown. These markets are rarely larger than American convenience stores, but they do a roaring trade in Cajun smokehouse specialties, such as smoked sausage, boudin and tasso, as well as store-produced spice mixes (see Pork and Spice Mixes in the Staples & Specialties chapter).

Hebert's Meat Market in the tiny Acadiana town of Maurice is a prime example. It routinely attracts customers from at least as far away as Lafayette with their many poultry and pork specialties. This is the place to procure thick pork chops stuffed with crawfish étouffée, cornbread stuffing, or flavorful rice dressing.

Liquor Stores

Unlike the bordering states in the American South, Louisiana has relatively permissive liquor laws. Consequently you can find an assortment of alcohol at almost every grocery or convenience store. For a better selection – and cheaper prices – go to a dedicated liquor store. These free-standing establishments tend to resemble supermarkets in both presentation and scope – extensive wine selections and a bartender's ransom in spirits await.

SHOPPING

JOHNSON'S GROCERY

There's a saying in Cajun Country: the best boudin is never more than three miles from home, but people make an exception for Johnson's Grocery. Customers have been coming to this little grocery and meat market in Eunice since 1937 to buy their boudin and other smoked specialties. In fact dedicated lovers of Johnson's boudin drive all the way from neighboring Texas for their favorite pig-based treat.

Fresh boudin is made here early every morning (except Sunday) and as you can imagine, they have the method perfected. The previous day, pork is browned then stewed over a low heat until tender. The juice is then drained from the meat and put aside. The green seasonings are prepared (green bell peppers and green onions), rice is measured out and placed in pots ready to be cooked first thing in the morning.

Before dawn, the lights come on in Johnson's Grocery and the boudin production begins. Pork liver is browned, the previously cooked pork is removed from the bone and is then mixed with the cooked rice. The meat and rice mix is put through a grinder with green seasonings, cayenne pepper, salt and black pepper. Once ground, this mixture is placed in a pressurized vessel, which feeds it into sausage casings made from pig intestines. When the boudin is boiled, it is ready to eat.

It's sold by the pound and by the plump, half-pound link. Although the chewy skin of the boudin is completely edible, most people prefer to squeeze out the tasty filling and discard the casing.

But the work at Johnson's Grocery isn't over once the boudin is made. There are other items that need to be prepared for a stint in the smokehouse behind the store. Pork specialties such as tasso, pounce and andouille are prepared and left in the smokehouse alongside turkey wings and ham hocks. It's an eerie sight, seeing all these different cuts of meat hanging from hooks in the hazy interior.

On Saturday mornings, the queue of customers starts at the meat counter right at the back of the store and snakes out the door. There are local folks as well as out-of-towners, all here to buy their weekly supply of boudin and other meaty specialties. Johnson's Grocery has to make boudin twice on a Saturday because the first batch is always sold out by 11am.

Charmaine O'Brien

Johnson's Grocery, where the locals come to buy their boudin, Eunice

Specialty Shops

With food and fiery condiments ranking high among Louisiana's exports, you will find a large number of tourist-style stores that specialize in the food products of the area. These stores usually traffic in kitchen equipment and kitschy souvenirs as well as food, so expect homespun chotskies (little souvenirs) along with your kitchen wares. The shelves of specialty shops are crammed with canned gumbos, packets and jars of seafood boils, Creole mustard, canned or vacuum-packed coffee and chicory, beignet mix, King cake kits, packaged pralines, packaged seasoning mixes, filé, local cookbooks, dried beans, local rice, regional meals in a packet (just add water) and zillions of hot and barbecue sauces.

Thanks to a recent widening of grocery distribution, travelers from the US may recognize some of the these formerly Louisiana-specific products. Others – especially some of the more extreme pepper sauces – are developed to cater to a tourist trade rather than the locals. Either way, let your personal tastes be your guide, and rest assured that when purchased in Louisiana, these products have better Cajun pedigree than those purchased elsewhere. This is especially true for local specialties like filé, local honey, and fruit jams and jellies.

As an added convenience, many of these places will pack and ship these wares to your home – for a price. This practice is also common to local seafood and meat stores that cater to the tourist trade.

K&B PURPLE

In 1998, a much loved New Orleans commercial institution, the K&B Drug stores, fell victim to a thoroughly unpopular corporate sellout. Founded in 1905, the New Orleans-based Katz & Bestoff (K&B) empire grew 180 drug and grocery stores in six states and inspired fierce loyalty among New Orleanians. Equal parts pharmacy, convenience mart, and liquor store, the K&B splashed its trademark color (called, surprisingly enough K&B Purple) on its store decors and everything from prescription drugs to playing cards. The inexpensive house brands of ice cream and less-than-premium vodka were standards in freezers and liquor cabinets throughout New Orleans. Generations of local school children started school with shocking purple notebooks and matching pencils. But after 93 years of business, the K&B era came to an end when the chain was purchased by a universally-despised Midwestern Conglomerate Which Shall Not Be Named (no endorsement here). Some die-hard locals still weep bitter tears when purchasing non-purple drugstore merchandise. Even from beyond the corporate grave, K&B purple is in their blood.

Markets

Even though you may be a non-cooking traveler, a local farmer's market offers you a chance to see regional produce before it hits the kitchen. Unfortunately, fresh food markets have become increasingly rare since the supermarket revolution. Gone are the days when the New Orleans French Market thrived as a fresh produce market, where New Orleanians bought their daily supplies. At the modern-day French Market, you are more likely to buy a pair of sunglasses or a bottle of hot sauce than a bunch of bananas just off the boat from Honduras, or **mirlitons** (vegetable squash) fresh from local fields.

There are local farmer's markets to be found, however, and these are worth hunting out. These markets are the places to buy local produce, and the person running the stall is often the person who grew or made what they are selling. This is where many locals do their shopping as, unlike supermarkets, the produce available here is the pick of the season. New Orleans has a farmer's market every Saturday morning (see the boxed text The French Market later in this chapter). Look in the local paper or ask at the local chamber of commerce to find out if there is a farmer's market operating when you are visiting the smaller towns.

Vegetables at the French Market, New Orleans

THE FRENCH MARKET

It was once possible to buy everything you needed to feed a household at the French Market. But when I arrived here early one morning in eager anticipation of my senses being assailed with the color and vigor that marks a great food market, I was sorely disappointed.

Perhaps I had the wrong place, or there was a part of the French Market that I had missed. Well, I was not in the wrong place. After making my way through the sunglasses stalls and those selling silver jewelry from India and sarongs from Indonesia, I finally found the fresh produce section of the French Market.

Officially called the Farmer's Market, it is housed in the larger complex of the French Market. As I got closer all I could see were shelves and shelves and shelves of hot sauces, beignet mix, cans of coffee and chicory, more hot sauces and a huge display of local-style instant meals.

I persisted, and found three stalls of fresh produce where there were a few tomatoes, strawberries, peaches, a small selection of faded vegetables, and watermelons stacked in piles. There were a few ropes of garlic, wreaths made from hot peppers, and piles of packets of pecan nuts. There was also a small seafood stall selling fresh and frozen seafood. Nevertheless, this was a market that had no intention of feeding the locals, and instead sold mostly manufactured products to tourists.

The French Market has been operating in New Orleans since 1791. The early French settlers attempted to meet their own food needs by growing vegetables and fruit trees and keeping a cow in the backyard. When the Spanish took control of the colony they said phooey to the idea of doing it yourself and planned a big central market where everybody could buy and sell their produce. So the idea of a city market took hold.

The location of the market sat on an old Native American trading site, and in the earlier days of the market, the Native Americans came here to sell fresh sassafras leaves and the wild game that they had caught. By the late 19th century the market stalls lined the Mississippi River, where an armada of boats docked to be loaded and unloaded. Some of this early cargo was food products from other climes. Refrigeration had not yet been invented so people shopped daily and bought only their household needs for the day to avoid spoilage. With the unerring flow of produce, the market became a cacophony of colors and smells, and was described by artist-naturalist John James Audubon as the "dirtiest place in all of the cities of the United States."

The present location of Café du Monde and the adjacent row of shops selling T-shirts and voodoo charms was once the site of the Halle des Boucheries, the huge meat market where German butchers sold sausages and cured meats.

As food transportation moved away from sea to air and rail freight and refrigeration became a reality in every household, the need for such a huge central market dissipated. Then someone came up with the concept of a supermarket and slowly, the French Market shrank – the present site that the market occupies is only a fraction of its former size.

Folks who live in the French Quarter expressed anger when the city council further reduced the size of the market in favor of commercial development – a betrayal of the city's traditional lifestyle in the interest of tourist dollars. Even so, you should visit the French market as you can still see the older architectural features and buy a punnet of fresh strawberries or a whole watermelon.

Weighing mushrooms at the Crescent City Farmer's Market

On a more positive note, there is a great fresh-produce market in New Orleans that is well worth a visit if you are there on a Saturday. The **Crescent City Farmer's Market** (700 Magazine Street, open 8 am-noon) is housed in an old garage. While it is not huge, it has a wide array of fantastic fresh produce and homemade goodies. All the stalls at this market are run by the growers or makers, so you can ask all the questions you want about the five varieties of squash they are selling or about making fruit wine or cooking live crabs, or how to cook fresh red beans or okra or hot peppers. You can also buy freshly ground filé, pepper and cornmeal here.

The produce sold at this market is seasonal, so what is available will vary, but the quality is always top notch. Many local chefs shop at this market and take the opportunity to get to know local suppliers.

As well as selling fresh produce, the Farmer's Market can cater to on-the-spot cravings. So go with an appetite and enjoy a fresh fruit pie and a cup of homemade strawberry lemonade. Otherwise pick up a loaf of freshly baked bread, a piece of local cheese, a pound of Creole tomatoes, a jar of pickled eggs, a few pieces of fresh fruit and head to the riverside for an impromptu picnic.

Charmaine O'Brien

SHOPPING

A New Orleans Picnic

Louisiana has the perfect climate for outdoor dining, and its many parks and riverbank spaces lend themselves to improvised alfresco meals. Just remember when planning any outdoor eating that it rains here nearly every afternoon at the height of summer.

Many local specialties are designed for outdoor eating. If you're near the French Quarter, swing by one of the Italian groceries on Decatur Street and pick up a gargantuan muffuletta – a great self-contained picnic food – along with the appropriate side dishes (locally-made Zapp's potato chips and a frosty Barq's root beer). Next head over to the French Market for a punnet of oversized strawberries, then find an open spot along the riverfront to munch while the mighty Mississippi makes its way to the sea.

STANDARD EQUIPMENT

Since most roads in Louisiana eventually lead to good food, denizens of the Bayou State generally drive with styrofoam or insulated ice chests (also known as coolers) in the car. The reason is simple: you never know when you'll find yourself miles from home with fresh, perishable foods. During travels across the state, it's standard practice to stop at remote small towns to stock up on local produce and specialties. Whether stocked with fresh-peeled crawfish in Breaux Bridge, smoked sausage outside of Scott or icy cold beer for a fishing trip, these ice chests never stay empty for long.

In a similar vein, substantial poboys are available throughout the state, ready for quick lunches on the go. If you're picnicking with a group, grab a few with different fillings – fried oyster or barbecued beef from a local grocery would be perfect – and a six-pack of Abita beer. A sweet praline or two to 'assist your digestion' wouldn't hurt either. Then take the St Charles Avenue streetcar to Audubon Park, which was formerly a sugar plantation (the first in the region and the home of Etienne Boré, who discovered the process for granulating sugar). Find yourself a comfortable spot under the sheltering oaks in this lush city park. After you have eaten take a digestive hike through Audubon Zoo or the stately campus of Tulane University.

If you like your poboys dressed, you may want to be cautious with mayonnaise during summer months. Dig into your sandwich as soon as possible after buying, as prolonged heat can cause the popular condiment to spoil with unpleasant digestive consequences.

Johnny's Po-Boys, St Louis Street in the French Quarter, New Orleans

Boiled seafood makes great picnic food, so find yourself a full-service seafood market and buy some boiled crabs, crawfish or shrimp. Most seafood suppliers have a light that flashes when a batch of boiled seafood is ready. If you are buying crabs, don't forget to take something with you to crack the shells, such as the heavy end of a table knife. Beer (Dixie will do) is the requisite drink to accompany this feast and don't forget a healthy handful of napkins. Find a spot by the water, spread out some newspaper on the ground or picnic table and enjoy the messy mealtime of champions. Post-meal handwashing is advised for this picnic option (see Boiling Points in the Where to Eat & Drink chapter).

Most restaurants will also package their plate lunches or regular foods 'to go' in styrofoam takeaway boxes. Rather than enjoy all your meals indoors, ask a diner or country restaurant to pack you up some food: fried chicken, potato salad, cornbread, stewed green beans and some freshly baked fruit pies. Grab an iced tea and find a quiet riverside spot for a lazy post-meal snooze.

SHOPPING

Things to Take Home

To make it easier to recreate some of the dishes you have enjoyed, try to take some local products home with you. Specialty stores, supermarkets, and even souvenir stands make it easy for you to stock your kitchen with the requisite tools and ingredients.

What you take home with you depends on where you live and how you intend to travel home. If you live in the US your options are wide open. Visitors from outside the US will be restricted by customs regulations, and it is a good idea to check details before you go.

Cookbooks

First you have to know *how* to cook these dishes, so a good cookbook is always a smart purchase. The recent popularity of Cajun and Creole cooking make for a floodtide of Louisiana titles, so take the time to browse through to make sure they feature your favorite dishes. Check this book's Recommended Reading section for some suggested titles.

Seafood or Meat Products

Some folks will suggest taking home seafood products packed for flight, but we wouldn't wholeheartedly endorse this practice. Granted, the seafood purveyors in this region are experts at packing the stuff securely in dry ice and polystyrene foam. And sure, many seafood specialists can organize a take-home order of seafood for you. But the best part of the region's local seafood is its freshness – and dry ice doesn't do much for *any* food's freshness. Better to enjoy the sea critters while you're here and pine for it until your next trip.

Filé

Since this popular gumbo thickener is native to Louisiana, buy a jar of filé powder as a matter of course. You may not get another chance to stock up until your next trip to New Orleans.

Pepper Sauces
Thanks to the recent popularity of Louisiana pepper sauces, there are literally hundreds of different varieties ranging from the pleasantly spicy to the toxically inedible. Some of these fiery blends cater to chile heads with extreme tastes, so beware the designation of 'XXX' or some of the more macho label designs. Some of the local classics include Avery Island's Tabasco Sauce (now in a variety of heat levels and flavors), Trappey's Red Devil, Abbeville's popular Cajun Power Garlic Sauce, and St Martinville's Cajun Chef Sport Peppers.

Spice Mixes & Cajun Seasoning

These pre-mixed spice blends have the dual advantage of being delicious and easy to transport. No bottles to break, no sauces to spill. Locals swear by Tony Chachere's Cajun Spice or Konriko Seasoning. Even if you are not taking fresh seafood home take some seafood boil with you; if nothing else, the packaging is great (see Seafood Boil in the Staples & Specialties chapter). If you buy liquid seafood boil you can add it to lots of other dishes and a few drops is good in salad dressing.

Roux
Inexperienced or impatient? You can buy roux in several prepared forms, including readymade or fat-free powdered roux. Even the locals consider this bit of 'cheating' somewhat legitimate – the flavor's authentic, even if the experience isn't.

Creole Mustard
Many New Orleans recipes call for this tasty whole-grain mustard, but it's tough to find outside Louisiana. If you're going to recreate the city's trademark remoulade sauce, spring for a big jar of Zatarain's (the most popular local brand).

Pralines
These sweet delectable treats are great for last-minute impulse buys. If you are travelling long distances, buy them gift-wrapped but if you're closer to home buy them fresh from any store's countertop. The biggest challenge is not to eat them all before you get home.

SEASONAL FRUIT & VEGETABLE GUIDE

Use this seasonal guide to assist you in the search for the best regional produce. Knowing seasonal availability will also help guide you when ordering from menus.

WINTER

December	January	February
collard greens	collard greens	collard greens
fava beans	fava beans	fava beans
green onions	green onions	green onions
mustard greens	mustard greens	mustard greens
turnip greens	turnip greens	turnip greens
winter squash		

Vegetables at the French Market, New Orleans

SPRING

March
collard greens
fava beans
green onions
mustard greens
turnip greens

April
collard greens
mustard greens
turnip greens

May
Creole tomatoes
eggplant
mustard greens
okra
summer squash
sweetcorn

SUMMER

June
bell peppers
collard greens
Creole tomatoes
eggplant
hot peppers
mustard greens
okra
peaches
summer squash
sweetcorn
watermelon

July
bell peppers
Creole tomatoes
eggplant
figs
hot peppers
okra
peaches
sweetcorn
watermelon

August
Creole tomatoes
eggplant
hot peppers
muscadine grapes
okra
peaches
red beans
summer squash
sweetcorn

FALL (Autumn)

September
collard greens
Creole tomatoes
eggplant
green onions
mirliton
muscadine grapes
okra
red beans
summer squash
watermelon
winter squash

October
collard greens
Creole tomatoes
eggplant
green onions
hot peppers
mirliton
mustard greens
okra
pecans
red beans
summer squash
sweet potatoes
watermelon
winter squash

November
collard greens
Creole tomatoes
eggplant
fava beans
hot peppers
mirliton
okra
pecans
red beans
sweet potatoes
winter squash

Cast-Iron Cookware

For the strong and/or determined, cast iron cookware makes a great purchase. After all, you can't make a good roux without one. Find a hardware store and choose from dutch ovens (for roux and small gumbos), 10-inch skillets (for morning eggs or smothering pork chops) or smaller frying pans (for small batches of perfect cornbread).

Boiling Rigs

If you're really serious about wanting to cook the large format foods of Louisiana (boiled seafood, deep-frying turkeys) then you could purchase the complete boiling rig, which includes a burner, large pot, strainer and wooden paddle. But to be honest, this kind of capital purchase is most feasible if you are travelling by car, as butane tanks don't fit under airline seats and customs officials tend to bristle when you declare quasi-industrial cooking equipment. Nevertheless, a stirring paddle made of cypress wood makes a great stand-alone gift.

Local Coffee & Other Beverages

Cans of chicory coffee (Café Du Monde is the local brand) or shrink-wrapped bricks of Louisiana dark roast (Community Coffee is the best) make good presents, especially if you could add a packet of beignet mixture to replicate the famous New Orleans breakfast. A bottle of potent New Orleans Rum or local wine are both good portable options, but be aware of customs regulations.

Louisiana Music

You know the saying, "when in Rome, buy the local music." Any New Orleans cooking session needs an appropriate soundtrack, whether it's hard-driving zydeco rhythms, a smooth Cajun accordion waltz or classic New Orleans rhythm and blues (see the boxed text Soundtrack Suggestions in the Louisiana Gumbo Party chapter).

a louisiana
gumbo
party

For many travelers and food enthusiasts, the natural *joie de vivre* of a Louisiana meal can be downright infectious. After you've sampled fresh-shucked Gulf oysters or a hearty gumbo, you'll be wanting to relive the experience whenever possible – both on your travels and in your own kitchen.

Once you return home, you'll want to do more than just *tell* friends about the foods of New Orleans, you'll want to *serve* friends the foods of New Orleans. Luckily, recreating the culinary atmosphere of Louisiana can be fairly simple, even if you're continents away from the Bayou State.

One key to a successful Louisiana food party lies in choosing the right food for your celebratory feast. How about a traditional New Orleans feast in the old-school Creole style? That would be great, if you're prepared to cook six or so different courses and shine up your 'special occasion' silverware. When they were still commonplace, these complex banquets required hours of cooking, a lot of maintenance and a brigade of chefs in the kitchen. Better to try something simpler.

Or how about treating your friends to a down-home Cajun crawfish boil? Not likely, or terribly practical, since the high quality live crawfish are tough to come by outside Southern Louisiana. The temperamental critters are tough to come by even in the neighboring state of Texas. Besides, there's also the complications of huge butane burners, giant pots, and tanks of flammable compressed gas. Better to try something more user-friendly.

The perfect solution for the 'cook at home' Louisiana experience is, of course, a nice hearty pot of gumbo. Think about it: gumbo is the most adaptable food in the Louisiana culinary pantheon. It appears on menus everywhere from the restaurants of New Orleans' Bywater District to the plate lunch eateries on Acadiana's Bayou Teche. You can find authentic varieties of gumbo based on poultry, seafood, wild game or even vegetables, if you consider the Lenten specialty **gumbo z'herbes** (green gumbo). An inherently versatile dish, gumbo can be thickened with filé, slices of fresh okra from the garden, or a deeply-browned roux. Gumbo is a favorite in the Louisiana kitchen as it lends itself to whatever ingredients are on hand, and it caters well to informal get-togethers with family and friends. If you've got a few hours to cook and a powerful need to celebrate, a Louisiana gumbo party is always in order.

Start off by doing a little research and playing to your home region's culinary strengths. If you live where seafood is plentiful, cook up a gumbo with crabmeat, shrimp, or even plump oysters. Plant lovers can use their garden's bounty to flavor the pot. Finned fish aren't usually prime ingredients for gumbo – that would make it a Cajun **courtboullion** – but you can start off with a plump chicken, a few wild ducks or part of a roasted turkey and end up with a wonderful gumbo. If any local butcher shops specialize in spicy smoked sausage, throw that in as well. Keep in mind that the gumbo is now doing what it does best: adapting to *your* environment.

Once you've assembled the ingredients for your own local gumbo, contact a group of your friends and buy your favorite local beer (lots of it).

Louisiana Chicken & Okra Gumbo

Ingredients

⅔ cup	neutral-flavored oil (for the roux)	1 tsp	ground white pepper
⅔ cup	flour (for the roux)	3	garlic cloves, crushed
10oz (300g)	tomatoes, diced	2	chickens, cut into quarters
6 cups	cooked rice	1	small onion, peeled
2 cups	fresh okra, sliced	1	large red bell pepper, diced
6 cups	chicken stock	1	large green bell pepper, diced
2 tblsp	Tabasco sauce	2	onions, diced
2 tblsp	tomato paste	2	stalks celery, diced
5 tblsp	Worcestershire sauce	1	bay leaf
2 tsp	dried thyme leaves		sea salt to taste
2 tsp	dried oregano leaves		freshly ground pepper to taste
1 tsp	ground cayenne pepper		filé powder
			pepper sauce to taste

Here's a gumbo that you can make almost anywhere. If you want to get exotic, use duck instead of chicken and slice a couple of pounds of spicy sausage in at the end.

Simmer the chickens in 8 cups (2L) of water with the garlic cloves and the small onion for about an hour. Remove the chicken parts from the pot and discard the garlic and onion. Skim all the fat from the chicken stock. If you have the time, the easiest way to do this is to put it in the refrigerator overnight and lift off the solidified fat in the morning. When the chicken has cooled, remove the meat from the bones and discard the bones and skin.

In a heavy soup pot that will hold at least 8 quarts (8L), make a dark brown roux with the oil and flour (see the roux recipe in the Staples & Specialties chapter).

When the roux is the desired color, turn off the heat and add the peppers, onion and celery, sauteing until the vegetables are soft (about 5 minutes). Add the tomatoes, Worcestershire, Tabasco, tomato paste, bay leaf, thyme, oregano, cayenne, and white pepper. Stir thoroughly. Slowly whisk in the skimmed chicken stock a little at a time, making sure there are no lumps. Cook over a medium heat for 30 minutes. Add the okra and chicken meat and continue cooking for another 30 minutes. Season with salt and pepper as required. Remember, the gumbo should be fairly thick.

To serve, mound a half a cup of rice in the middle of a bowl. Ladle gumbo around the rice. Serve with pepper sauce and filé powder.

Makes 12 servings

Robb Walsh

The same goes for crusty French bread. Next comes the fun part: the cooking. Ideally, you should have a leisurely Sunday afternoon solely dedicated to good food and good times. Choose one guest from your list who can tell a good story and get them slowly stirring the roux (if your recipe calls for one, that is). Crack open a beer and put on some appropriate music (see the boxed text Louisiana Sounds later in this chapter). As the roux slowly turns brown, talk with your partner in crime about pressing matters of the day, including your favorite local restaurant or memorable dishes from your childhood. Do a little shuffle around the kitchen as you chop, sauté and stir.

Later, as the pot burbles away on the stove, check the seasonings of your developing gumbo. Dip a wooden spoon into the pot, or soak up the flavor with a hunk of fresh French bread torn straight from the loaf. Adjust seasonings as necessary. Crack open another beer. Dance a little more, preferably to a smooth Cajun waltz.

By then, it'll be time for the rest of your guests to arrive. If you have some Louisiana memorabilia, such as Mardi Gras beads or souvenir doubloons, you can decorate with those, but the music and food should suffice. Casual, hard-eating exuberance is the most important element at any gumbo party.

If you're prone to serving starters, some shrimp remoulade can be prepared the night before (see the recipe). Guests can wash the critters down with a glass of cold beer. If your friends are cocktail fans, shake up the ingredients for a Sazerac (see the recipe in the Drinks chapter). Start cooking a big pot of rice on the stovetop. Change the music to up-tempo zydeco for a festive pre-meal soundtrack.

Prior to serving, everybody should be milling around the kitchen instead of sitting stiffly in the dining room. Invite the guests to lift the pot lid and take a peek at the ever-thickening gumbo. As the rice steams, throw a tablecloth over the table and grab a handful of spoons from the cutlery draw. Set out a couple of uncut loaves of bread, a selection of Louisiana pepper sauces and extra filé for sprinkling. Place a stack of bowls near the pot, and when the rice achieves fluffy perfection, it's time to serve.

Ask your guests to line up at the stove and hand them each a bowl. It's a 'serve yourself' affair and they can control the crucial rice-to-gumbo ratio. As they serve themselves, watch them stir and identify the various floating ingredients. "Is that a crab claw? How much sausage is in here, anyway?" Accompaniments should be simple. Lightly dressed field greens, thick-sliced tomatoes, or a classic chunky potato salad is always appropriate. As the group sits down at the table, put on an album by a smooth New Orleans crooner – anything by Johnny Adams would do nicely – and serve your own bowl. Pour another beer and let the meal begin.

As both host and cook, your work is nearly finished. The rest of the evening should be guided by talk of good food among good friends. "We had the best shrimp and egg stew at this little place in Maurice ..." You might like to alter the soundtrack to match the informal pace of the evening, faster or slower as the stories and second servings unfold. Cap off the evening with a dessert course of rich bread pudding or a simple pecan praline (see recipe later in this chapter). Or more beer. Maybe an after-dinner cocktail. It's easy to improvise.

Shrimp Remoulade

This dish can vary widely from cook to cook in Louisiana. Some recipes call for a tangy tomato base with plenty of horseradish for zing, while others prefer a smoother mayonnaise base. In either case, this New Orleans classic requires the freshest shrimp available, preferably from the nearby Gulf of Mexico.

Ingredients

2 tblsp	Creole mustard
1 cup	good mayonnaise
1 tblsp	cayenne pepper
3 tblsp	celery, finely chopped
½ cup	green onions (scallions/spring onions), finely chopped
1 tsp	garlic, crushed
1 tsp	parsley, finely chopped
1 tblsp	prepared horseradish
	cayenne pepper, salt and black pepper to taste
2 tblsp	lemon juice
2lb (1kg)	shrimp, peeled and cooked

To serve

iceberg lettuce, torn
tomatoes, cut into wedges
hard-boiled eggs, sliced
black olives
lemon wedges

Combine all the ingredients (except the shrimp) in a bowl and mix well. Set in the refrigerator for at least 1 hour.

When ready to serve, gently mix the shrimp through the sauce. Serve on a bed of lettuce, and garnish with tomato, egg and olives. Serve with a lemon wedge.

Serves 8 as an appetizer

The Red Room on St Charles Avenue, New Orleans

SOUNDTRACK SUGGESTIONS

As with the food, the music you'll hear on your travels in Louisiana will be of the home-grown variety. The musical traditions of the region are enjoyed by locals and visitors alike, and form the musical backdrop for local festivals and street dances. Here's a short 'cheater's guide' to help you tell a Cajun 'two-step' from a New Orleans 'second line'.

Rhythm & Blues (R&B) – Smooth voices and thumping rhythms characterize the local version of this 20th-century African-American style. Standout acts include Irma Thomas, Johnny Adams and Ernie K Doe.

New Orleans Funk – The modern synthesis of the city's rhythms and complex musical tradition with an infectious, rump-shaking thump. The omnipresent Neville Brothers are the global ambassadors of this form, but don't overlook greats like the Funky Meters, Galactic, or George Porter, Jr.

Zydeco – This Francophone music is a fast-dancing adaptation of modern R&B fronted by accordion and **frottoir** (washboard) for added percussion. A good rule of thumb from telling this style from Cajun music is this: if a song sounds vaguely like Ray Charles' "I Got a Woman", it's pure zydeco. Class acts include Geno DeLaFose, Beau Jacques and the Zydeco High Rollers, Boozoo Chavis, Rosie Ledet, and Clifton Chenier, the late great unchallenged king of zydeco.

Brass Bands – This is a New Orleans tradition that can include everything from peppy traditional Dixieland to hard-driving contemporary jazz with pronounced bebop and hip-hop rhythms. This energetic style is usually heavily percussive because of the city's informal 'second line' drumming tradition, where enthusiastic locals danced down the parade routes following the 'official' festivities. Recommended artists include: the Dirty Dozen Brass Band, Rebirth Brass Band, Little Rascals Brass Band.

Cajun Music – This French take on traditional country music is an Acadiana standard, with accordion and fiddle (violin) in the lead and a washboard providing rhythm. This school of music is also called 'chank a chank' for the steady rhythm of the old-school songs. Contemporary groups have updated the music with more modern instrumentation and musical influences, but there's still a deep respect for the 'old songs', and the accordion is still right up front. Good bets include Beausoleil, Savoy-Doucet Band, Filé, Steve Riley and the Mamou Playboys.

New Orleans Piano – The Crescent City is justifiably famous for its keyboard tradition, from the Mardi Gras standards of Professor Longhair to the barrelhouse rolls of James Booker to the modern tones of voodoo man Mac 'Dr John' Rebennack. Local boy turned pop star Harry Connick, Jr cut his teeth on New Orleans piano jazz.

Pecan Pralines

Creoles believed sugar improved digestion after a meal, and a popular way of taking it was as a crunchy pecan praline. Today you'll see pralines everywhere – New Orleans has a number of stores that specialize in making them and they are also sold at roadside stalls, restaurants, local diners and general stores.

Ingredients

2 cups	pecan halves
3 cups	light brown sugar
	a pinch of salt
¾ cup	evaporated milk
1 tblsp	butter

Toast the pecans in the oven over a medium heat or in a skillet until they give off a nutty aroma (careful not to burn them).

Mix the sugar, salt, milk and butter in a heavy-based pot over low heat. Cook, stirring constantly, until the sugar is dissolved and the mixture is smooth.

Increase the heat to medium and add the pecans. Stir constantly until it has reached the soft-ball stage (a couple of drops of the hot mixture dropped into a cup of cool water forms balls). Remove from the heat and beat for about 2 minutes.

Drop a teaspoonful of the praline mixture at a time onto a foil-covered or greased tray. When they have cooled gently lift each piece from the foil with a knife. Store in an airtight container.

Makes about 24

Charmaine O'Brien

fit & healthy

You shouldn't encounter any serious health problems in New Orleans as long as you're sensible. The water is clean, special vaccinations aren't required, and a wide and varied diet is available. The health problems you may encounter are likely to be either digestion or hangover related.

Water

The tap water in New Orleans is safe to drink, although not particularly tasty. As a matter of preference rather than necessity, locals in the city shy away from tap water, and instead drink bottled water.

For the visitor, there are many relatively inexpensive brands of bottled water that are available wherever soft drinks are sold. In a restaurant setting, tap or filtered water is automatically placed on the table. Poor-tasting water may also affect the taste of drinks made with it, and not for the better either.

Diarrhoea & Constipation

If you find yourself with a dose of diarrhoea the likely cause is either the change of diet or too much rich food or drink. In just about every town you will find a supermarket-style pharmacy (Walgreen, Eckerd's, and Rite Aid are common names) or a local pharmacy. These establishments generally have ample supplies of over-the-counter anti-diarrhoea preparations. Long opening hours are the norm for these stores and a pharmacist is usually available for consultation. If diarrhoea persists, seek further medical advice.

The receptionist at your hotel will be able to point you in the direction of a local medico.

Ironically, you may experience constipation for exactly the same reasons that you may experience diarrhoea. The same pharmacies will have products (either chemical or fiber-related) to help ease such a malaise. There is also a wide range of antacid products to help ease various forms of heartburn and indigestion.

Praise the Lard
Pigs feature prominently in Louisiana cooking, and rendered lard is used extensively in frying and pie crusts. If pig is not your preference, check the food you ordered isn't fried or made with pork products.

Heat & Dehydration

Louisiana has a semi-tropical climate, and during the summer months of June, July and August, the heat can get to even the most stalwart traveler. If you plan to visit during this time, be prepared to sweat. Temperatures of 100°F (37.8°C) and readings of 100% humidity are not as uncommon as locals would like.

Consequently, you should aim to constantly rehydrate – drinking water (beer and coffee don't count) whenever possible, but especially after physical exertion. Dehydration is potentially very dangerous, but easily avoidable. Don't be caught out by the heat. Avoid outdoor activities in the middle of the day and always wear a hat and sunscreen while on your wanderings.

Children

There are no specific health concerns for children. The above information is just as relevant to children as to adults. Lotions and potions are readily available to treat the usual childhood ailments (insect bites, stings, sunburn).

Do not ever leave your child unsupervised in a car – heat exhaustion is dangerous and potentially deadly. The same rule applies for pets (no offense intended).

Kids waiting for a drink at the Crescent City Farmer's Market, New Orleans

Allergies

If you suffer from a food allergy, you know what you can and can't eat. Be sure to ask if you're unsure what is in a dish, or check with the kitchen staff – you are your own best protection. With that in mind here are a couple of hot spots we identified:

If you are allergic to *any* seafood, always double-check with your server before digging in. It may not be listed on the menu but shrimp goes into many dishes chopped in small chunks, or is used as stock.

If you have a wheat or gluten allergy, don't just chow down on cornbread as it is typically made with some wheat flour. Also check the origins of any soup or sauce as they are quite often thickened with a roux (a mixture of flour and oil). Again, better to ask than react.

If you are allergic to nuts, particularly pecans, be especially vigilant when ordering desserts or dishes that have a stuffing, as nuts are a favorite ingredient in both.

Diabetics

As a diabetic you know how to best manage your individual condition. There are, however, two points that will be of interest in your travels.

First, much of the food here has a high fat content. Boiled seafood is a good low-fat (but high-salt) option, as is most blackened seafood – but be careful of the ever-present butter sauce. When you order a salad ask for dressing on the side, and be aware that servings can range from extra large to immense.

Second, you should not have any trouble eating regularly as many restaurants and cafes are open from early morning to late evening. On Sundays, however, establishments are often not open or operating to limited hours.

Recommended Reading

Amil, N. *Peppers: A Tale of Hot Pursuits* (1989)

Time–Life Books *American Cooking: Creole and Acadian* This book is about 30 years old but it still holds up. Lots of great colour pictures of Deep Southern life in 1970.

Edgerton, J. *Southern Food* (1987)

Fitzmorris, T. *The Eclectic Gourmet Guide to New Orleans* Alabama, Mehasha Ridge Press, Inc. (1996) A great, unpretentious guide to eating in New Orleans.

Fry, M. & Posner, J. *Cajun Country* Pelican, Gretna (1999) If you really want to understand and explore Cajun country then this is the book for you.

Guste, R. *100 Greatest Dishes of Louisiana* W.W. Norton & Co., New York (1988)

Prudhomme, P. *Chef Paul Prudhomme's Louisiana Kitchen* (1984) The book that started the Cajun trend.

Toole, John Kennedy *A Confederacy of Dunces* Random House (1980) Probably the most recommended comedic novel about New Orleans, with a special nod to the ever-present Lucky Dog carts.

Bienvenu, Marcelle *Who's Your Mama, Are You Catholic, and Can You Make a Roux?* Times of Acadiana Books (1991) Anyone interested in Cajun food will love this collection of stories and family recipes from one of Louisiana's best food writers. This book is a perfect balance between a family album and heirloom recipe box.

Fowler, Damon Lee *Classical Southern Cooking* Crown Publishers (1995) A good overview of Deep Southern food culture as it developed through history. Well researched with plenty of good recipes.

Talk about Good!: Le Livre de La Cuisine de Lafayette Junior League of Lafayette (1994)

River Road Recipes, The Textbook of Louisiana Cuisine Junior League of Baton Rouge (1959) Classic texts of Louisiana home cooking.

Gutierrez, C. Paige *Cajun Foodways* University of Mississippi Press (1992)
A thorough academic analysis of Cajuns and their foods.

Bilbe, Ruth and Kornman, Naomi *Come to the Mardi Gras* T.I.N.S. Press, New Orleans (1999) This little fold-out book gives a thumbnail sketch of Mardi Gras traditions past and present.

Web Sources

www.bestofneworleans.com The site of *The Gambit Weekly*, New Orleans' alternative weekly newspaper. Use it to keep track of the local entertainment and restaurant scene.

www.nomenu.com The frequently updated reviews and musings of local restaurant maven Tom Fitzmorris, who also has an informative radio show covering the New Orleans food scene. Always informative, with an amazing depth of knowledge.

www.gumbopages.com A labor of love from New Orleans expatriate Chuck Taggert, currently a resident of Southern California. Covers the ins and outs of general New Orleans culture.

READING

Photo Credits

Jerry Alexander Front cover, p1, p9, p12, p13, p21, p27, p29, p30, p33, p34, p35, p36, p39, p40, p42, p43, p44, p45, p46, p47, p48, p49, p51, p52, p54, p55, p56, p60, p61, p63, p64, p66, p70, p71, p72, p73, p74, p75, p77, p78, p79, p80, p81, p82, p83, p85, p88, p89, p91, p94, p96, p98, p100, p101, p103 top right, bottom, p104 p107, p108, p109, p112, p117 top right, bottom left, p124, p135, p136, p139 left, bottom right, p143, p148, p150, p151, p152, p153, p154, p157, p158, p159 right, p165, p166, p168, p169, p170, p171, p172, p173, p176, p177, p179, p180, p181, p184, p185, p187 top, bottom left, p188, p189, p190, p191, p192, p193, p195, p197, p199, p200, p201, p202, p205, p212, p213 top left, bottom right, p215, back cover.

Lee Foster p16, p20, p24, p117 bottom right, p118, p123, p139 top right, p144.

Olivier Cirendini p5, p8, p103 top left, p106, p114, p146, p187 bottom right, p213 bottom left.

John Davison p10, p86, p128, p140, p210.

Richard Cummins p92, p117 top left, p121, p159 left, p160.

Neil Setchfield p14, p133.

Margaret Jung p213 top right.

Rick Gerharter p122.

A

absinthe bitter, anise-flavored green liqueur that contains oils of wormwood. Thought to drive people to madness and suicide, it was banned in the early 20th century. Today anise-flavored liqueurs such as Pernod or **Herbsaint** are substituted for absinthe.

Acadiana another name for southwest Louisiana's Cajun Country, short for 'Acadian Louisiana'

Acadians another name for Southern Louisiana's **Cajun**s, originally French refugees from the Canadian maritime province of Acadie (now Nova Scotia). This group settled in the marshes and prairies of southwest Louisiana.

andouille smoked sausage made using pork and spices, most often used to flavor dishes

appetizer the first course of a meal

B

Bananas Foster trademark New Orleans dessert consisting of bananas sauteed in butter, brown sugar, and banana liqueur, then flambeed with high-proof rum

bayou slow-moving marshy river tributary commonly found in Southern Louisiana

beignet deep-fried square donut. Common and traditional as a New Orleans breakfast food, beignets are served liberally-coated with powdered (confectioner's) sugar, usually accompanied by **café au lait**.

Big Easy a recent nickname for New Orleans most often used by non-natives and marketing types. Use the phrase 'Crescent City' instead.

biscuit quick bread leavened with baking soda instead of yeast, common in the American South as a breakfast food

bisque smooth creamy soup of French origin, made from shellfish and stock made from their shells. In Louisiana it is made with **crawfish**, and garnished with stuffed crawfish heads.

bitters infusion of aromatic roots and herbs and used to flavor cocktails

blackened food that is quick-seared using a red-hot cast-iron skillet. A style of cooking made famous by Cajun chef, Paul Prudhomme.

black-eyed pea small, cream-colored bean that has a distinctive black 'eye', common to **Southern country-style cuisine** and **Soul Food**

black-iron skillet frying pan made of cast iron

boudin (blanc) Cajun sausage that is made with a mixture of ground pork, pork liver, rice and seasoning. It is boiled and served hot as a popular snack or breakfast dish.

boudin rouge rare variation of **boudin** made with the addition of pigs' blood.

bouillabaisse French seafood stew made with fresh fish, shellfish, olive oil, garlic and tomatoes

bourbon whiskey that is distilled from maize and rye, named after the county of Kentucky where it was first made

bread pudding favorite dessert in Louisiana, made of stale day-old bread, sugar, eggs and cream, often served with a bourbon-sugar sauce

brioche sweet, rich yeast bread, flavored with butter and eggs

broad bean see **fava bean**

brunch meal that falls between lunch and breakfast

butter bean see **lima bean**

buttermilk thick milk product, treated with special bacteria cultures to provide a tangy flavor, used in biscuits and cornbread

C

café au lait coffee mixed with hot milk

Cajun the Cajun people live in Southern Louisiana; their French ancestors came to Louisiana by way of Nova Scotia, Canada. The name Cajun derives from a mispronunciation of the word 'Acadian', a name by which the Cajuns are also known.

Cajun cooking draws its techniques from 300-year-old French cookery and its ingredients from whatever is available. Slow-cooked, highly seasoned, one-pot dishes define this cuisine

Cajun Country called Acadiana on the Louisiana state map, this area covers Southern Louisiana and ends in an apex just below Alexandria in the north of the state

cane syrup sugarcane juice that has been boiled down until it reaches the consistency of a thick syrup

carnival annual, pre-Lenten festival running from Twelfth Night (6 January) until **Mardi Gras** (the moveable feast also known as Shrove Tuesday). The whole carnival period is sometimes called Mardi Gras although technically speaking this refers only to the final day

chaudin pig's stomach that has been stuffed with the same mixture used to make **boudin**, then smoked

chayote see **mirliton**

chicory relative of endive; the root of chicory is roasted and ground and used as a coffee substitute. New Orleans coffee is typically a blend of 60 percent coffee beans and 40 percent chicory root.

chitlins the intestines of a pig, or pork tripe. A popular Soul Food dish.

chitterlings see **chitlins**

Cocktail Sauce a regular at oyster bars and **crawfish** boils. Mix your own cocktail sauce with ketchup, prepared horseradish, pepper sauce and lemon.

cornbread the simple, everyday bread most often seen on **Southern country-style cuisine** and **Soul Food** menus. Leavened with baking soda and baking powder instead of yeast, and cooked on campfire or stovetop as easily as in an oven.

country fried style of cooking either chicken, pork chops or well-tenderized steak. The meat is coated in either flour or breadcrumbs and cooked in a frying pan.

courir de Mardi Gras a horseback run-through held in Cajun Country on **Mardi Gras**. Bands of masked and costumed riders go from house to house collecting ingredients for a communal **gumbo**.

courtbouillon in Cajun cooking, a **roux**-based fish stew, rich with tomatoes, peppers and spices (pronounced KOO-be-yawhn)

cracklins pork skin cut up into small pieces and deep fried in rendered lard. Served seasoned as a popular snack.

crawfish resembling tiny lobsters, these crustaceans grow wild in the freshwater wetlands of Louisiana

Creole cookery the distinctive local cuisine of New Orleans, derived from classical French cookery and reshaped by the availability of ingredients, climate and various cultural influences. Rich and sophisticated, Creole cookery commonly features local seafood, complex sauces, and heavy use of butter.

Creole multi-faceted term that can describe languages, ethnic groups, or cuisine, depending on context (see the boxed text **Creole in Context** in the Culture chapter)

Creole Mustard flavorful, coarse-grained mustard common in Louisiana cooking

crustacean shellfish that has a hard external body (exoskeleton) and soft internal body. The shell is segmented and has legs. Examples include crawfish, shrimp and crabs.

D

dirty rice white rice cooked with chicken giblets, ground pork, green peppers, celery and seasonings, served as a side dish

dressed 'dressed' **poboy** sandwich comes with iceberg lettuce, tomato and mayonnaise

E

entree main course (US)

Epiphany Catholic church holiday. Celebrates the visit of the Magi (three kings) to the Christ child.

étouffée French for 'to smother'. A stew-like dish that can be made with shrimp, crawfish, or various meats. Always served with rice.

F

fais do do formerly a Cajun house dance, the term now refers to a large-scale street dance featuring Cajun or **zydeco** music

fava bean large, flat greenish-brown bean that is used both fresh and dried. Important to New Orleans' Italian community.

filé ground sassafras leaves used to thicken **gumbos**

fried pies a popular convenience dessert; flaky crust is wrapped around fruit or custard fillings, then plunged into boiling fat until the pie is crispy and hot

G

gens de couleur libres French for 'free people of color'; any of the black immigrants who came to Louisiana from 'free states' during the time of slavery. Many *gens de couleur libres* came from the French West Indies (Haiti, Santo Domingo) and settled throughout Southern Louisiana.

go cup a plastic cup used for the outdoor consumption of alcoholic drinks in New Orleans

gratons the Cajun name for **cracklins**

green onions also known as scallions or onion tops

grillades grilled slices of beef or veal that is stewed in a seasoned tomato sauce, served with **grits** as a common New Orleans **brunch** dish

grits coarsely ground **hominy** that is cooked into porridge and served at breakfast or as an accompaniment to meats

Gulf Coast the coastline of the American South that borders on the Gulf of Mexico

gumbo perhaps Louisiana's best known dish. A cross between a soup and a stew, it is thickened with a **roux** base, okra or **filé**, and always served with white rice.

gumbo z'herbes green **gumbo**, a Lenten specialty made with various leafy greens

H

Herbsaint yellowish licorice-flavored aperitif, Herbsaint is a locally produced **absinthe** substitute used in cocktails

hog's head cheese formless gelatinous sausage made with the meat from the jowl of the pig

hominy kernels of maize that have been softened and bleached using a lye and water mixture, often ground to make **grits**

hoppin' John rice and black-eyed peas

hushpuppy deep-fried balls of corn meal batter

J

jambalaya rice-based dish similar to Spanish *paella* or *arroz con pollo*. It usually includes chicken and sausage, though ingredients will vary according to what is available.

joie de vivre French expression meaning the joy of life or the love of life

K

kidney bean large, crescent-shaped bean, usually dark red in color

King cake brioche ring decorated with icing and colored sugar, traditionally served as a **Twelfth Night** holiday tradition. A small baby figurine is baked inside the cake.

L

la cuite extremely thick version of **cane syrup** with the consistency of taffy

Lent period of 40 days from Ash Wednesday to Easter eve which is devoted to abstinence and penitence to commemorate Christ's fasting in the wilderness. Before the rise of Christianity this period marked the time between the end of winter and the first spring crops.

lima bean kidney-shaped flat bean that is either pale green or white

Louisiana Pepper Sauce fermented mix of pepper pods, salt and vinegar

M

making groceries New Orleans slang for grocery shopping

maque choux dish made from fresh corn kernels, bell peppers (or onions) and tomatoes; believed to be an original Native American dish which was taught to the Cajuns

Mardi Gras Fat Tuesday, the day before Ash Wednesday. The final day of the carnival period which is celebrated with extravagant parades. A day of indulgence before the restraint of the **Lenten** period.

marsh soft, low-lying land often covered with standing water, common along the Louisiana coast

mayhaw crabapple-like berry found along river bottoms in Northern Louisiana

meuniere simple French sauce consisting of browned butter and a little lemon

mirliton vegetable squash native to Louisiana

molasses thick, black syrup that is the by-product of sugar refining. It is rich in minerals.

Muffuletta another New Orleans original, this enormous sandwich is filled with Italian cold meats, cheese and spicy olive salad

P

panee to pan fry

parish an administrative subdivision in Louisiana that is the equivalent of a county in other US states; another vestige of Catholicism

pignolatti special fried pastries common to local Italian celebrations of the Feast of St Joseph. These bready pastries are shaped like the pine cones that Christ allegedly used as childhood toys.

Pimm's Cup cooling cocktail made with Pimm's No. 1, a gin-based aperitif, and ginger ale garnished with lemon and cucumber

plate lunch set menu lunch usually consisting of one meat dish and three vegetable dishes and bread, although it may also include a drink and dessert

poboy French bread split and stuffed with any number of fillings. Fried oysters, soft shell crabs and roast beef are popular. The official oversized sandwich of New Orleans.

pompano popular saltwater fish caught in the Gulf of Mexico, a member of the jack family

ponce pig's stomach that has been stuffed with the same mixture used to make **boudin**, then smoked

praline rich sugar and pecan confection found throughout the Deep South (pronounced PRAW-leen in Louisiana)

R

red beans and rice bean stew made with red beans and pork, always served with rice. A classic Monday dish in New Orleans.

red fish fine moist-fleshed fish found in the Gulf of Mexico. When 'blackened' redfish became a popular Cajun dish, overfishing caused the depletion of the Gulf fisheries.

red gravy Italian-influenced tomato-based sauce used in New Orleans cuisine

remoulade classic spicy **Creole** sauce served with cold shrimp or other shellfish, made either with a mayonnaise or tomato base

rice dressing see **dirty rice**

roux thickening agent made from wheat flour browned in butter, lard or oil; the base of **gumbo** and various other sauces and soups

S

sauce piquante spicy and versatile tomato-based stew often flavored with **roux**, a standby in Cajun cookery; not to be mistaken for the Mexican *salsa picante* (a cold tomato-and-pepper sauce)

seafood boil boiling bag containing a blend of bay leaves, mustard seeds, cayenne pepper, peppercorns, cloves and allspice

smothered long-cooking style similar to braising, in which meat or seafood is browned and cooked in flavorful gravy

snowball see **snow cone**

snow cone shaved ice drizzled with brightly-colored, flavored sugar syrups

Soul Food the food of the African slaves, developed out of necessity but still very popular for its rich, deep flavors. Uses a lot of fat and spices.

Southern country-style cooking the style of food the American settlers brought to the Deep South, whose roots lie in English cookery

T

tasso lean pork that has been rubbed with spices and smoked. It is used in small quantities to flavor dishes.

turkey bone gumbo rich **gumbo** made from the carcass of a roasted turkey, a typical Cajun post-Thanksgiving dish

Twelfth Night see **Epiphany**

V

Vieux Carre French for 'old square', an alternative name for the French Quarter, the original settlement of New Orleans

Y

Yat trademark accent of New Orleans and the people who speak it. A combination of Italian-American, Irish-American and African-American dialects, the Yat accent sounds remarkably like New York's 'Brooklynese'. From the common salutation 'Where y'at?' ('How's it going?')

Z

zydeco fast-dancing Francophone adaptation of modern R&B fronted by accordion and washboard (*frottoir*) played as percussion, common in southwest Louisiana

Recipes

More World Food Titles

Brimming with cultural insight, the World Food series takes the guesswork out of new cuisines and provide the ideal guides to your own culinary adventures. The books cover everything to do with food and drink in each country – the history and evolution of the cuisine, its staples & specialities, and the kitchen philosophy of the people. You'll find definitive two-way dictionaries, menu readers and useful phrases for shopping, drunken apologies and much more.

The essential guides for travelling and non-travelling food lovers around the world, look out for the full range of World Food titles including:

Italy, Morocco, Mexico, Thailand, Spain, Vietnam, Ireland, Turkey, France & Hong Kong.

Out to Eat Series

Packed with independent, unstuffy opinion on hundreds of hand-picked restaurants, bars and cafes in each city, Lonely Planet's Out to Eat guides take food seriously but offer a fresh approach. Along with reviews, each Out to Eat identifies the best culinary cul-de-sacs, explores favourite ethnic cuisines, and the food trends that define each city. They also serve up the nitty-gritty on dish prices, wheelchair access and other useful facts with each review, and all include useful quick-scan indexes.

Updated annually, Out to Eat titles cover:
Melbourne, **Sydney**, **London**, **Paris** and **San Francisco**.

Planet Talk

Our FREE quarterly printed newsletter is full of tips from travellers and anecdotes from Lonely Planet guidebook authors. Every issue is packed with up-to-date travel news and advice, and includes:

a postcard from Lonely Planet co-founder Tony Wheeler
a swag of mail from travellers
a look at life on the road through the eyes of a Lonely Planet author
topical health advice
prizes for the best travel yarn
news about forthcoming Lonely Planet events
a complete list of Lonely Planet books and other titles

To join our mailing list, residents of the UK, Europe and Africa can email us at go@lonelyplanet.co.uk; residents of North and South America can do so at info@lonelyplanet.com; the rest of the world can email talk2us@lonelyplanet.com.au, or contact any Lonely Planet office.

The Lonely Planet Story

Lonely Planet published its first book in 1973 in response to the numerous 'How did you do it?' questions Maureen and Tony Wheeler were asked after driving, bussing, hitching, sailing and railing their way from England to Australia. Written at a kitchen table and hand collated, trimmed and stapled, *Across Asia on the Cheap* became an instant local bestseller.

Eighteen months in South-East Asia resulted in their second guide, *South-East Asia on a Shoestring*, which they put together in a backstreet Chinese hotel in Singapore in 1975. The 'yellow bible', as it quickly became known to backpackers around the world, soon became the guide to the region. It has sold well over ¾ million copies and is now in its 10th edition, still retaining its familiar yellow cover.

Today there are over 400 titles, including travel guides, walking guides, language kits & phrasebooks, travel atlases & maps, diving guides, restaurant guides, first time travel guides, condensed guides, illustrated pictorials and travel literature. The company is the largest independent travel publisher in the world.

The emphasis continues to be on travel for independent travellers. Tony and Maureen still travel for several months of each year and play an active part in the writing, updating and quality control of Lonely Planet's guides.

They have been joined by over 120 authors and over 400 staff at our offices in Melbourne (Australia), Oakland (USA), London (UK) and Paris (France). Travellers themselves also make a valuable contribution to the guides through the feedback we receive in thousands of letters each year and on our web site.

The people at Lonely Planet strongly believe that travellers can make a positive contribution to the countries they visit, both through their appreciation of the countries' culture, wildlife and natural features, and through the money they spend. In addition, the company makes a direct contribution to the countries and regions it covers. Since 1986 a percentage of the income from each book has been donated to ventures such as famine relief in Africa; aid projects in India; agricultural projects in Central America; Greenpeace's efforts to halt French nuclear testing in the Pacific.

Lonely Planet Offices

Australia
Locked Bag 1, Footscray, Victoria, 3011
☎ 03 9689 4666
fax 03 9689 6833
email: talk2us@lonelyplanet.com.au

USA
150 Linden St, Oakland, CA 94607
☎ 510 893 8555 TOLL FREE: 800 275 8555
fax 510 893 8572
email: info@lonelyplanet.com

UK
10a Spring Place, London NW5 3BH
☎ 020 7428 4800
fax 020 7428 4828
email: go@lonelyplanet.co.uk

France
1 rue du Dahomey, 75011 Paris
☎ 01 55 25 33 00
fax 01 55 25 33 01
email: bip@lonelyplanet.fr